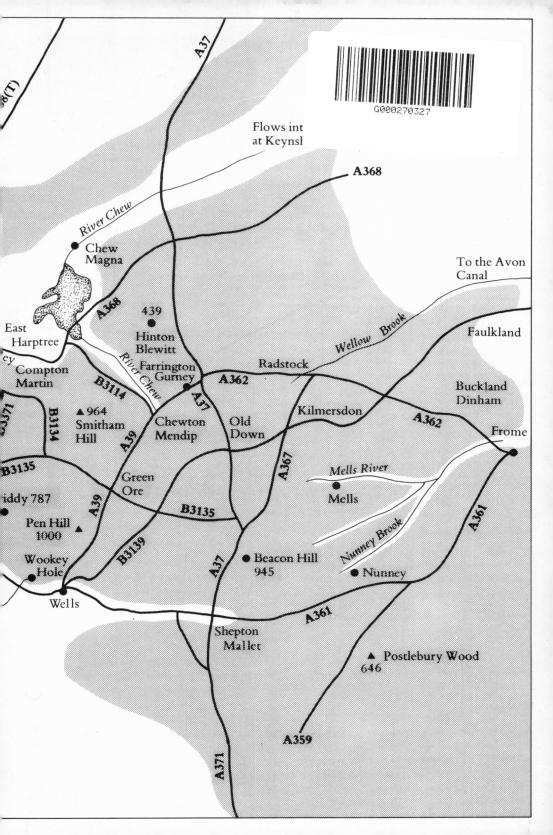

THE MENDIP HILLS
A Threatened Landscape

THE MENDIP HILLS

A Threatened Landscape

by

SHIRLEY TOULSON

LONDON
VICTOR GOLLANCZ LTD
1984

ACKNOWLEDGEMENTS

The following copyright material has been used: "Mendip" (p. v) from *The West Country Magazine*, 1948, reprinted by permission of the poet, Robin Atthill; the verses on pages 145 and 146 were collected by Ruth L. Tongue in *The Chime Child* (1967), reprinted by permission of the publisher, Routledge & Kegan Paul; the poem on page 122 by Richard Cox Gough is reprinted by permission of Mr Donald Gough; the verse on page 137 is reprinted by permission of Sidcot School; the verse on page 141 is from *Catch This*, the parish magazine of Axbridge, Shipham and Rowberrow. I am most grateful to these people for allowing me to use their words.

S.T.

British Library Cataloguing in Publication Data
Toulson, Shirley
  The Mendip Hills.
  1. Mendip Hills (England)—History
  I. Title
  942.3'83   DA670.M5
  ISBN 0-575-03453-X

Typeset at The Spartan Press Limited, Lymington, Hants
and printed in Great Britain by
St Edmundsbury Press, Bury St Edmunds, Suffolk.
Illustrations originated and printed by Thomas Campone, Southampton

MENDIP

The steep walls climb from the stifled valley
to the limestone crags, barrier to a strange world,
where the dead buried their dead in the humped
barrows along the ridge in the pagan summer.
The brown grass whispers the cruel wind;
from the sea creeps in the ships' low moan
fog-bound on the flats — a dead winter world.
Our fathers smelted what the Romans left,
grooved deep in the sunless hill, tortured
the darting streams to wash their precious ore,
scarred the smooth uplands, till their chimneys
crumbled and fell beside the glossy slag.

Here in a wind-screened hollow, turfed with thyme,
echoes faintly the voice of unquiet streams
that tumble far below in the vaulted rock.
The rough hill smiles; its pride of beauty
outdares desolation, cruelty, and death.
Lambing-time is bell-music in the blue-
veined wind of western spring; the year unfolds
in the crumpled bracken, the tiny green
of the heather, before the purple summer tide
breaks on the barrows of the hazy dead;
and O the climbing lark, whose harebell song,
as delicate as clear in sunburnt March,
remembers all my yesterday on the dry-
walled lonely hills that stride to the Severn Sea.

ROBIN ATTHILL

CONTENTS

ILLUSTRATIONS

Following page 44

Western Mendip: Burrington Combe and Blackdown *(photo West Air Photography)*

Strawberry pickers, *circa* 1905 *(photo Collection Bill Parsons)*

The Model Farm at East Harptree *(photo Richard Raynsford)*

Priddy Sheep Fair *(photo Shirley Toulson)*

A wild bee wall at Lower Farm, Charterhouse *(photo Shirley Toulson)*

St Andrew's Quarry, Doulting, which provided the stone for Wells Cathedral in the twelfth century, and the new quarry beside it *(photo Shirley Toulson)*

Batt's Combe quarry, above Cheddar, making as great a scar in the hills as the natural gorge *(photo West Air Photography)*

Gruffy Ground: Ubley Rake at Charterhouse *(photo John Cornwell)*

Writhlington Colliery near Radstock, 1968 *(photo John Cornwell)*

The ruins of Fussell's iron works at Mells *(photo John Cornwell)*

Following page 108

Wells Cathedral from the Bishop's Meadows *(photo Shirley Toulson)*

Vicars Close, Wells: the fourteenth century houses of the Vicars' Choral *(photo Gill Markey)*

The Norman pillars of Compton Martin church *(photo Gill Markey)*

Stone heads at the south door of Compton Martin Church *(photo Gill Markey)*

Ernie Small with truckles of Cheddar cheese in the 1940s *(photo Collection Bill Parsons)*

Hannah More: the good angel of Shipham, Rowberrow and Cheddar *(photo Collection Bill Parsons)*

ix

Richard Cox Gough, discoverer of the most famous show cave in Cheddar Gorge, with some of his large family (*photo courtesy of his grandson, D. W. Gough*)

The floods at Cheddar Gorge, 1968 (*photo courtesy of D. W. Gough*)

The bridge at Chew Stoke (*photo Gill Markey*)

A lead miner's buddlehouse in Biddlecombe, West Horrington (*photo Patrick Kirkby*)

Emborough Manor: part of this farmhouse dates from the thirteenth century, making it the oldest house on Mendip (*photo Shirley Toulson*)

Mill workers' cottages built into the side of the hill at Darshill, Shepton Mallet (*photo Shirley Toulson*)

Water from the Sheppy channelled to form part of the ornamental landscaping of Dinder village (*photo Shirley Toulson*)

One of Fussell's Italianate grottos by his pleasure lake at Chantry (*photo Shirley Toulson*)

The gentle face of Mendip: the southern slope at Axbridge (*photo Ian Ballard*)

Where the millennia meet: the ancient seabed separating the dolomitic and conglomerate limestone at Vallis Vale, Frome (*photo John Souster*)

Coppicing in the Somerset Trust for Nature Conservation's reserve at Asham Wood (*photo David Lester*)

Underneath the hills: cavers in G. B. Cavern, Charterhouse (*photo Nick Barrington*)

MAPS

ACKNOWLEDGEMENTS

MANY OF THE people who gave their time and experience to helping me with this book appear in its pages. I should like to express my deepest thanks to them for their patience with my questions and for their generosity in allowing me to take part in their understanding of different aspects of the Mendip hills.

Other people have been no less generous in helping me with their scholarship and advice. I should like to record my most sincere gratitude to Sir William Rees-Mogg as President of the Mendip Society; to Martyn Brown, formerly curator of Somerset's Rural Life Museum in Glastonbury; to Ann Heeley, also associated with that museum, whose work in recording the memories of retired farmers is nationally known; to Claire Austin of the Somerset Vernacular Research Group; to Frances Neale, on whose scholarly knowledge of the Saxon charters of the area, and of the history of the fairs and markets of Mendip towns, I have relied extensively; to J. B. Smith of the University of Bath for his assistance on customs and dialect; to Bill Butcher and Rob Jarman of the Somerset Naturalist Trust; to Hugh Lucas, the County Minerals Officer, Ken Painter and Rory Graham of Foster Yeoman and to Lady Violet Powell for talking to me about the recent history and future projects of the quarries; to Lord Hylton and Andrew Aldritch of the Hugh of Witham Foundation; to George Donkin of the Radstock Co-operative Society; to Philip Vennor of the Axbridge Office of King Miles estate agents; to Richard Raynsford for his explorations of the old roads and paths around Shepton Mallet; to Eunice Overend for her knowledge of the history and ecology of the Frome area; to Phoebe Rees for her work on the folklore of Somerset; to David Hales for his research into the history of the Mendip Motor Car; to Donald Gough, one-time curator of the Motor Museum in Cheddar and grandson of the man who opened Gough's cave to the public; to Tom Elkin, a recent warden of the Field Studies Centre at Charterhouse; to Lady Sarah Wright; and to Roy Lewis for patiently reading and checking the typescript.

The local history societies of Axbridge, Banwell, Frome and Shepton Mallet have provided me with much invaluable information. I should like to acknowledge my indebtedness to the enthusiastic work of their members.

I alone am responsible for any errors of fact or misinterpretation of information which may inadvertently appear in this book.

S. T.

PROLOGUE

The Mendip Hills: the Rocks they are Made of

IT IS ONE of those perfect days in late March that restore your faith in the coming summer. Warmed by the sun, a newly arrived chiff-chaff sings on a thornbush on the sloping northern side of Brean Down, the headland that juts out to sea to the south of Weston-super-Mare. On the shallow turf of the steep cliffs on the other side of the down, the brilliant blue of minute forget-me-nots rivals the cloudless sky. It is low tide and flocks of sheld duck are feeding on the glistening mud beneath the headland.

To the west are the aptly-named islands of Steep Holm and Flat Holm, and beyond them the Gower peninsula and the coal measures of South Wales. They are all part of the same fold in the earth's crust that formed the great mountain range, over three miles high, which towered across this part of Britain, millions of years ago. It eroded down to form the Mendip hills, which probably owe their name to the Celtic word for "rock", *maen*.

Like Brean Down itself, these hills rise steeply from the low-lying country to the south, where the rushy waters of a shallow inland sea covered the Somerset levels until men began to drain it in the tenth century. Curving north-west/south-east across Somerset and the new county of Avon, the hills have an average height of 800 feet, exceeding a thousand at some points. The high Mendip plateau is fifteen miles long, four miles wide from Compton Martin in the north to Draycott in the south. To the west of Blackdown it has eroded, leaving a series of isolated ridges, of which Brean Down is the last point on the English mainland. To the south-east the limestone ends in coal measures covering some 68 square miles, a small proportion of which was exploited in the Radstock area from the fourteenth century to the closure of the mines in the 1970s.

Between Brean Down and Radstock a convergence of geological processes has shaped a landscape of dramatic variety, culminating in an intricate folding of rocks. In this way the towering limestone cliffs

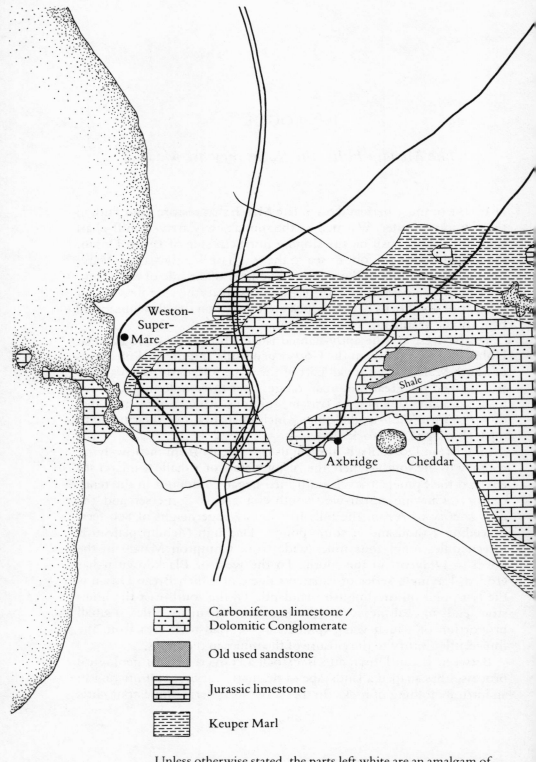

Weston-
Super-
Mare

Shale

Axbridge

Cheddar

Carboniferous limestone /
Dolomitic Conglomerate

Old used sandstone

Jurassic limestone

Keuper Marl

Unless otherwise stated, the parts left white are an amalgam of
Trias and Lias to the east, and alluvium around Weston-super-Mare.

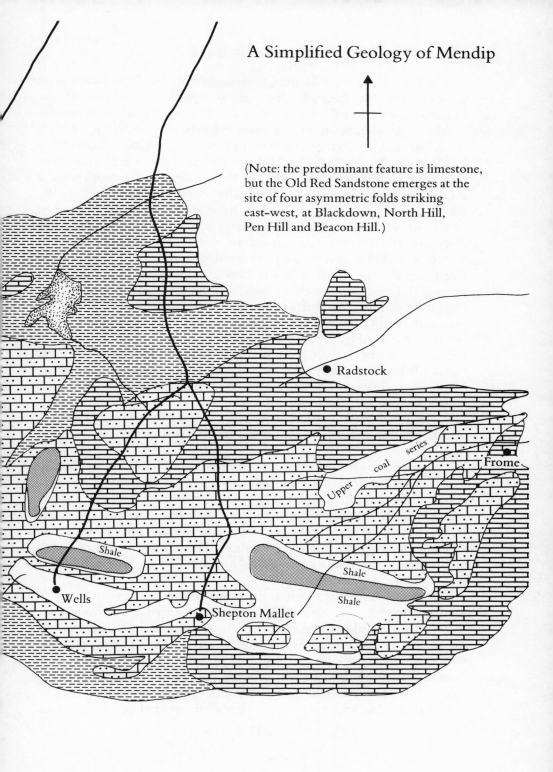

A Simplified Geology of Mendip

(Note: the predominant feature is limestone, but the Old Red Sandstone emerges at the site of four asymmetric folds striking east–west, at Blackdown, North Hill, Pen Hill and Beacon Hill.)

Radstock

Upper coal series

Frome

Shale

Shale

Shale

Wells

Shepton Mallet

of Cheddar Gorge were formed, and the stratified walls of Burrington Combe. On the heights, dry valleys follow the course of the limestone, occasionally enhanced by circular, man-made dew ponds.

Although Mendip is in the main a limestone landscape, with a small but classic pavement on Brean Down, its four highest points — Blackdown, North Hill, Pen Hill and Beacon Hill — are made up of the more ancient red sandstone, for the folding of the rocks pushed the older, impervious sandstone to the surface. In these places, the short springy turf natural to the limestone cliffs gives way to bracken and heather growing on beds of deep, rich peat. On the southern slopes of Beacon Hill, the sandstone is covered by lias limestone which stretches towards Shepton Mallet, and which provides the flagstones for the floors of many Somerset houses of any age. The ground to the south-east of the hills, around Doulting, is made up of the cream-coloured limestone, of which the present Wells cathedral was built, eight hundred years ago. At the eastern edge of the region, the rock exposed by two quarries reveals the history of the hills for millions of years. A walk through the woods beside Mells river from Great Elm ends at the quarry face of Vallis Vale, where a time chart of stone is uncovered for all to see how the triassic dolomite conglomerate formed long after the the layers of carboniferous limestone had been flooded. A mile or two to the east, at Tedbury camp, you can actually walk on the old sea bed that formed on the first limestone.

The use of this stone for virtually every building put up on Mendip before the start of this century, and for very many of them afterwards, is one of the main attractions of the area. It is also a cause of one of the major problems that people concerned with the conservation of the hills have to face, for in some places the quarries that provide the stone threaten to remove them altogether. The threat becomes more insistent now that the stone is needed not so much for local building as for surfacing the nation's roads.

Of course, human exploitation of the land is no new thing. The man-made landscape of Mendip began to be formed in the Stone Age. Advanced technology makes change more rapid and irrevocable, but the men who lived in caves in these limestone cliffs around 8000 BC would gladly have contributed to the extinction of the beasts they hunted if their equipment had been up to it, and if the vast climatic changes that took place in that era had not been more effective.

When the Mendip caves were first rediscovered in the last two centuries, they were found to be stocked with the bones of the animals who roamed these hills long before men ventured to live here. Hippopotamus and hyena, cave lion, leopard and lynx, mammoth, woolly rhinoceros and reindeer once inhabited the territory where herds of Friesian cattle and hardy cross-bred sheep graze today. The largest hoard of bones from the vanished creatures was discovered around 1800, when miners, looking for the lead sulphate and zinc carbonate which have been extracted from the rock for centuries, came across a great cavern full of animal remains near Banwell, four miles to the east of Weston-super-Mare. Although no horse bones were discovered in that find, they were quite commonly included among the later deposits in Mendip caves. So it is reasonable to assume that the people of the Bronze Age, who built the barrows which still mark the high ridges, and the Celts, who came after them and who raised extensive earthworks to make their hill forts which guarded the crossing points of the high ground, had horses to help them in their work and battles.

It was these Bronze Age and Celtic peoples, with their improved tools, who accelerated the clearance of the primeval forests, first begun by neolithic farmers. The process of clearance went on speedily and continuously from Celtic and Roman times to the late nineteenth century, as the lead miners used more and more timber in the furnaces where the ore was smelted. Hence many of the Mendip heights are unwooded, except for the relatively ephemeral acres of Forestry Commission pines and firs, which appear to kill the land they exploit. The optimistic view is that these conifers will eventually check the course of erosion, and in a few centuries produce sufficient topsoil to support the deeper rooted, indigenous broad-leafed trees. That is something I have to take on trust, for to me the ground between the close growing trees seems sadly and permanently dead.

True growth may eventually come out of the commercial forests, but the land of the old lead mines is irredeemable, although it does sustain enough life to make it interesting to naturalists. The scars which the lead mines have left on the western slopes of Mendip are more substantial and unalterable than the coal batches (tips they are called elsewhere) in the east, which are steadily being planted over and transformed into quite shapely man-made hills.

The lead miners of the eighteenth and nineteenth centuries left shallow pits rather than batches as a record of their work. These remain as "gruffy", or groovey, ground on the high plateau around

Charterhouse and Priddy. These are the places where the uneven ground is so rough and full of such dangerous dips that it is quite unsuitable for grazing, even if the traces of lead which still linger in the soil did not constitute an even more insidious hazard to the beasts.

The difference between the mining activities and their remains in the west and east of Mendip is a reflection of the basic contrasts in this landscape. The divide of the region comes at the impressive geological folding between Cheddar and Wells. To the north and west is the Mendip plateau, fringed by the steep inclines of the hills; to the east the contours are for the most part much gentler. The stone walls give way to hedges, and the farms enjoy more sheltered conditions, although they are not immune to the mists and low cloud which so often envelop one part or another of the hills. For the weather on Mendip can alter within a mile or two, and a traveller on the M5 or the A38, which bisect the western section of the hills, may well experience quite different conditions within minutes. One consistent factor is that growth on the Mendip plateau is always a month behind that on Somerset levels and the land sheltering under the southern scarp of the hills, which has long been used almost exclusively for market gardening.

The contrasting localized climates have always contributed to the various uses that people have made of the region, and the different ways in which they have fashioned the landscape, differences which have been exaggerated to the point of farce. I have even been asked to believe that from the studies of the marks found on the teeth of the paleolithic skulls exhumed from the caves, archaeologists have concluded that while Cheddar man in the south brushed his teeth with a frayed twig, the people of Burrington Combe, a few miles to the north, picked theirs with a pointed one. Yet however they cleaned their teeth, by the time their remote Bronze Age descendants inhabited Mendip it is pretty certain that the heights were more populous than they were to become in historic times. It was not until the advent of general motoring came to lessen the isolation of the hills that people chose them as a pleasant place to live. Even now there are only two fully settled hilltop villages: Priddy in the south and Hinton Blewitt to the north.

Sparse as its own population has been in the past, Mendip has always supplied one essential need of the cities of Bristol and Bath, which now virtually form one conurbation. It is from Mendip that the cities get their water. Indeed rain that fell on the hills over five thousand years ago is responsible for the purest thermal springs at Bath; but the more mundane water supply comes from the vast lake created by the drowning of the Chew Valley just after the war. Several other reservoirs also contribute to the needs of the cities, and many of these waters have a subsidiary leisure use. Anglers and bird watchers are watched in their turn by the summer picnickers, and these people are joined by the growing numbers of city workers who prefer to live in the country, and who are turning many north Mendip villages into dormitory suburbs.

From the eighteenth century people have chosen the Mendip villages for their retirement; but it is easy transport that has made the hills into an increasingly popular recreational centre. Walkers, riders and cavers all take their toll of this landscape, even if they do no more than compress the soil. Yet the damage they do is minimal compared to the mechanical havoc wrought by the quarries and the proliferation of ugly and thoughtless building. Mendip is under threat, and in writing about the people, past and present, who have shaped this landscape, I hope that I can establish the unique and vulnerable character of these hills, whose frail wild beauty could all too easily become submerged in a featureless suburban sprawl interspersed with "leisure parks".

PART ONE

THE WRITING ON THE LAND

CHAPTER I

The Farms

THE RIVER CHEW rises magnificently. It bounds out of the rock behind the neat cottages that climb the hill to the north of Chewton Mendip village; and immediately its waters are channelled to feed the pipes of the Bristol Water Authority. But that is a fairly recent story. For it was not until the 1950s that Mendip farms could rely on piped water. Before that time all the water that was needed for the farms surrounding the dry Mendip plateau had to be taken in carts from the springs to the fields and yards.

Even now you cannot be long in these hills without being aware of the paradox of water. The place is wet and misty, it boasts an annual rainfall of 45 to 50 inches; and yet, apart from occasional flooding, there is no standing water to be seen, and the rivers, which run underground for miles, would elsewhere be called brooks when they do eventually surface. The farms which have dictated the human pattern of this landscape are sited by springs or wells and for centuries the cattle were watered from carefully made circular ponds, which prevented rain and dew from seeping through the porous rock.

Yet, although water takes hard work to manage, it is plentiful and always has been. Stories abound of springs that never failed, even in the historic droughts, stretching back in time from the dry year of 1976. There is even a fresh water spring on the island of Steep Holm. It emerges from a water course that runs under the floor of the Bristol Channel, between that island and the mainland, and which, according to fishermen's tales, occasionally bubbles up to the surface through the salt waters. So Steep Holm has been farmed at least since the Iron Age, and the trace of other early field patterns on Mendip all relate to the proximity of a water supply. It was the lack of water that caused the high plateau of Mendip, now carefully marked out by the dry stone walls built two hundred years ago at the time of the enclosures, to be left for centuries as a barren wasteland. The Domesday survey found a ring of small villages round upland

3

Mendip, with only Wells and Chewton Mendip able to support more than ten plough teams.

Yet all the villages had grazing rights (or "sleights" as they are still called) on the bare uplands, marked by the barrows where the farmers of the Bronze Age buried their important dead, and with which they made their own waymarks across wild country. So traditionally the farmer at Barrow Farm, which stands across the road from the source of the Chew and beneath the long barrow whose grassy mound marks the sharp ridgeway at the southern edge of the plateau, had grazing lands around the Nine Barrows of Priddy, some five miles away. And the farms at Easton, beneath Mendip's southern cliffs, had grazing land which ran up to the heights of the cleft in the limestone at Ebbor Gorge. These farms on the fringes of Mendip had a double advantage, for they also held grazing rights and allotments on the lowlands, which stretch to Wedmore from the south side of the hills, and to Congresbury from the north.

Place names and scraps of buildings remain as evidence today of the village pounds, where animals which had no right to be on the common land were folded until their owners claimed them. They are witness to some of the disputes which went on about who was allowed to graze where. Some of these conflicts reached more than local proportions. In the middle of the sixteenth century a certain Robert May tried to exclude the commoners from Charterhouse Down on west Mendip on the excuse that the land had once belonged to the monks of Witham (some twenty miles to the east), where he had recently purchased land. His claim led to such friction that a map of Mendip showing all the commoners' rights was drawn up.

One of the difficulties was, and still is, that most of these pastures are fit for summer grazing only. Indeed the whole county gets its name from the fact that it provides rich summer pastures. Winter is another matter, with the lowland pastures under water, and the hilltops bleak and bare once the grass stops growing. So even now there are few cattle to be seen on Mendip fields in winter, which makes a pleasant respite for the walker who may not care for being followed along a public footpath by herds of inquisitive bullocks, but which is costly for the farmer who has to keep his beasts expensively housed and fed in stalls. In the past, it was this situation which provided a way of controlling the commoners' grazing rights, for farm tenants were only allowed to turn out as many animals each summer as they could reasonably expect to feed over winter.

Anyone with any sizeable herd of cattle or flock of sheep had to employ a cattleman or shepherd to keep an eye on the animals on the distant pastures. In the 1920s, when travelling was harder than it is now, telephones an expensive luxury, but the post still a swift and reliable service, it was quite usual for the Cattleman at Priddy to send a postcard to Barrow Farm, Chewton Mendip, to announce that a cow had calved. Life on "this once dreary mountain", as the Reverend William Phelps, an early nineteenth-century local historian, described Mendip, can still be bleak even in summer; and those who undertook the work of looking after the animals had to be paid for it in addition to their normal wage. Manorial accounts of the fourteenth and fifteenth centuries show that a shepherd who had to work on Mendip could expect 3s 4d in addition to his annual wage of 26s 8d.

There are still plenty of sheep to be seen on Mendip, hardy breeds which lamb successfully twice a year, so that it is quite usual to see newborn lambs in November. These lambs are now reared for the butcher. But when England's wealth lay in wool much of it came from the Mendip hills. The fleeces were sheared from a particular breed of sheep which no longer exist, but which are thought to have been something like Cotswold or Exmoor sheep. John Billingsley, an eighteenth-century agricultural reformer, who lived at Ashwick near Shepton Mallet, predicted the extinction of these small, hardy, fine-wooled Mendip sheep. He thought highly of the breed, describing it as being of "a sort that will thrive on the poorest soil, and fatten on such land as hardly keep other sorts alive". So he was sorry to see it declining in favour of the Dorsets and South Downs. In the fourteenth century the Bishop of Bath and Wells kept over fifteen hundred sheep on Mendip, grazing between Wrington in the north, Mells in the east and Batcombe in the south.

At that time the land was unenclosed, and with only a few exceptions the dry stone walls of western Mendip and the quickset hedges of the more undulating east were unknown. John Billingsley, who lived from 1774 to 1811, was the chief architect of Mendip's enclosures, arguing that by this method he could increase the numbers of sheep that could be stocked on upland farms. He dealt sharply with the simple, and mostly inarticulate, cottagers who had to lose their grazing rights on the hills to pay for the improvement. He even made a moral issue of the matter, declaring that a cottager who had the facility for grazing "a cow or two, or maybe some geese" could be tempted to put himself "above his brethren in the same rank of society"; worse

5

still "in sauntering after his cattle he acquires a habit of indolence," while the proceeds from the sale of his cow could lead to drunkenness. In contrast to such debauchery he predicted that the enclosed commons would prove capable of supporting "at least three times more stock than they did in a state of nature".

At about the same time (in 1796) a leading member of the newly formed Bath and West Society for the improvement of agriculture advocated a progressive home building policy for farm labourers' cottages "with the addition of a small piece of land" in order to prevent the drift to the towns at a time of great rural poverty. His additional argument was that neatness in his dwelling would also enhance the quality of the labourer's work for the landowner. It was a progressive view even if it may have been largely inspired by enlightened self-interest, for during this period of increased agricultural prosperity for the farmers, the labourers were so poverty-stricken that they were frequently reduced to stealing the turnips, grown under the new crop rotation schemes, in order to keep their families fed.

Meanwhile the prosperity of the Mendip landowners was such that they were able to draw in tenants from other counties reputedly in the vanguard of agricultural improvements, including one unsuccessful applicant from Thomas Coke's progressive Norfolk. These eighteenth-century innovations were mainly concerned with arable farming, and Billingsley accepted the challenge of producing a crop rotation for a countryside that had long been considered mainly pastoral. This meant urging farmers to manure and lime their land, which he believed would improve the quality of the ground tenfold. And in a manner reminiscent of the arithmetic exercises of my youth, he worked out that "4 horses and 2 men with 2 carts carrying 32 bushels of lime cover ½ acres a day if the lime kiln is not too far distant". The building of a good limekiln then cost about £10, and the stone remains of many of them can still be seen around Mendip today; others have vanished leaving only funnel-shaped depressions in the ground. The better-preserved ones were still in use in the 1920s. At the turn of this century farmers often used to burn their own lime, mixing it with sheep manure before putting it on the fields. Now on Mendip plateau two tons of lime per acre, used every four to seven years, are needed to grow crops such as kale, oats, dredge wheat and barley, which are mainly used for feeding stock, and the lime is mostly obtained from local quarries.

6

The increase in arable farming was also made possible by better ploughing. The implement traditionally used on Mendip was in Billingsley's opinion "the most awkward and ill-contrived that could be conceived". A new double-furrowed plough was introduced to the region, by a "speculative man", who had doggedly to prove its worth for ten years before anyone would follow his example. When it came to the harvest there were winnowing machines available, but the threshing was still done by flail. It was not until much later in the nineteenth century that the steam thresher came round to the farms. The machines had to be booked well in advance and a stock of coal and water made ready for getting up steam.

Even at the end of the century, when mowing and reaping machines were a common part of the harvest scene, scythes and sickles were still in common use. In Billingsley's time all mowing had to be done by hand. At least the work supplemented the casual labourer's meagre income; and as the corn on the hills ripened a fortnight later than that on the levels, the harvest stretched out a long time. Not everybody who wanted work could find it even then it seems, for Billingsley was able to make the complacent boast that there was never any shortage of hands for the work.

Those who did find work in the harvest fields were allowed, in addition to their wages, a ration of free beer: two gallons an acre for wheat, and one and a half for barley and oats. Billingsley does not mention cider, but many labourers expected a similar allowance of that drink, and most farms in the West Country produced their own. Mendip was no exception.

Cotton-wool-like in texture and virtually tasteless, cider apples grow in almost all parts of the region, and each farm had to produce enough liquor from them to keep its work force happy. The nineteenth-century teetotal movement did its best to combat this automatic consumption of intoxicating drink. In 1862 Thomas Gifford was awarded £1 and a special presentation certificate by the Glastonbury Agriculture Association for mowing 63 acres of grass without a drop of beer or cider. His feat was not widely emulated throughout Mendip.

Now the crops from the cider orchards, and many farms still have their own, are sold directly to commercial undertakings, who come with mechanical shakers to retrieve the apples from the trees. One of the best Mendip apple orchards has gone for ever, drowned by Bristol Waterworks' reservoir at Chew Valley. In the 1920s the farmer at

Barrow Farm, Chewton Mendip, who had come there from the lost hamlet of Moreton in that valley, tried to grow apples at Chewton Mendip. The attempt was a complete failure. He gave up in disgust and sold his apple trees for pit props. That story comes from his son, Walter Baber, a retired farmer himself now, who still supervises the orchard at the farm he built up at Stoney Stratton to the south of Shepton Mallet.

The making of good cider, in the old days, was hard work in itself, for the heavy apple crushers were still hand-operated well into the nineteenth century. Then the mushy pulp had to be put on the bed of the press between layers of barley straw. After the juice had all been squeezed out of it, the remaining apple-soaked straw (the *cheese*) was fed to the pigs and chickens, with disastrous results if fermentation had already begun.

That was not the only peril confronting the fowl at cider-making time. They will tell you that to make good Somerset cider, a newly killed hen, beak, feathers and all, had to be hung in the wooden cask where the juice was stored. Only when the acid had completely absorbed the carcass was the cider thought worth drinking. I have not proved whether that story is true or not, but it is certain that raw meat — beef or bits of rabbit — were frequently put into the cask to help fermentation.

Although the farmhouse cider that was produced by this method was often pretty rough stuff, the best of it was compared favourably to French wines by eighteenth-century connoisseurs. Nearly all the so-called farmhouse cider is commercially produced now in premises that are built for the making and distributing of cider, not for farming. They produce a potent, light-green, slightly honey-flavoured drink, and those who have a taste for it seek it out in pubs, like the Hunters' Lodge at Priddy, which some would claim to be the present heart of Mendip.

It is milk, not cider, that makes Mendip's money now. There have been many changes since the 1920s and early '30s, when the red and white roan shorthorns were milked in the open fields by milkmaids crouching on stools whose legs often sank into the ground in wet weather. These girls were no delicate figures of pastoral romance but stalwart ladies like Mrs Dyment of Litton, who used to milk for Walter Baber's father and who raised a large family as well as walking three miles each way for her twice-daily job. Milking was not only a job for women either; all farmers expected their sons to be able to milk. Hand milking is a skilled task, and when the Somerset farmers objected to the 1939 proposals to raise the school leaving age, it was because they felt that no boy could become a good milker unless he started before he was fifteen. Most of them started long before that. Walter Baber began milking when he was eight, and other farm children were expected to start on their fifth birthdays.

Dairy methods which had hardly altered for centuries began to change in 1933 with the first draft scheme for the Milk Marketing Board, which Somerset was the first county to adopt. This introduced legislation on tuberculin tested milk, and the fear of that disease still haunts Mendip. For in no other region has the badger been made such a scapegoat as a carrier of bovine tuberculosis.

At the outbreak of the Second World War the predominant farming enterprise on the hills was dairy cattle. It still is, with the herds of black and white Friesians, their numbers for the milk records branded on their buttocks, replacing the shorthorn Buttercups and Duchesses of a less mass-produced era. They still have precedence over everything else on the roads, however, as, accompanied by their attendant Hereford bull, they amble along bearing their heavy udders from field to milking parlour. The cars queue up behind them, and if the weather is bad it is as likely as not that their drover will be doing his work from one himself.

Beef cattle as well as dairy cows graze on Mendip in summer, for the hills have become a general stock for the rest of the country, and many bull calves that spend their first months here are sold to graziers in the north of England, East Anglia and Kent.

The raising of beef stock often goes with the cultivation of barley. Gordon Hendy, who farms with his father Tom in the south-east of the region near to the village of Faulkland, puts his land to both those uses. The farm they run has been in the family for generations, and that is how the senior Mr Hendy thinks it should be. "Farmers must be born and brought up on the land," he says, and is sorry when farms get into the hands of joint stock companies and conglomerates. Certainly his son has a feeling of continuity. College-trained and anxious to grow the best possible crops, using all the advantages of modern science, he is none the less mindful of the people who cultivated his acres centuries ago, perhaps growing some of the barley that has been found in the Mendip Bronze Age barrows. He talks with excitement of the Roman and medieval finds that he has made in his fields.

Mr Alfred Gay, who farms with his three sons at Eastwood Manor Farm in the village of East Harptree above Chew Valley lake, is another Mendip farmer who is continuously aware of the past. He could hardly fail to be, for his farmhouse dates from the fifteenth century, while his dairy cattle are stalled in a remarkable Victorian model farm steading. Stretching over one and a half acres, it bears a strong resemblance to Joseph Paxton's burnt Crystal Palace, even though the glass of this roof has now been replaced with perspex. The building was designed in 1858 by Robert Smith, agent of John and Frederic Knight, who had earlier astounded the county by building elegant farmhouses in the wilder parts of Exmoor. The Eastwood building was meant for the use of a barley and beef farm, which also grew a substantial crop of flax. It had two lavish covered cattle yards with a fountain playing in the centre of each one, stabling for over twenty horses, a piggery and a veterinary hospital adorned with stone carvings of farm animals. New times have led to new uses. The Gays are dairy farmers. There are no horses on the farm now, and the pigs are housed beside the old blacksmith's building, whose forge is still in working order. The main stabling has become the milking parlour, and one fountain has had to go; but the space for grain storage above the yards is still in use.

In contrast to these magnificent farm buildings, the Tudor farmhouse, mentioned by John Leland, in his report of his tour of Somerset in the mid-fifteenth century, as being of recent origin, only reveals its age to an eye practised in discerning the features of old buildings, for it has been modernized to suit the convenience of generations of farming families. It was obviously originally built by someone of wealth and standing, most probably the Sir John Newton of nearby Richmont castle, which is now merely a wooded mound.

Other Mendip farms have disappeared as completely as Sir John Newton's proud castle, which played its part in the twelfth-century wars when Stephen succeeded in capturing it from Sir William de Harptree, who was holding it for Matilda. Of much later date is the crumbled ruin, almost completely hidden by the dense sea buckthorn and alexanders of Steep Holm. It is the remains of a farmhouse built in the 1830s and farmed some 40 years later by Frederick Harris and his family. They were succeeded in 1885 by a Caroline Davies and her two sons, who took over the island farm and provided most of their own food, as well as feeding an eight-man garrison stationed there to ward off any invasion threats. The Davieses kept five heifers and one steer as well as goats, pigs and a donkey. The latter was used as a draught animal to haul stores up the steeply winding path from the harbour to the flat top of the island. During this century the island was farmed for a little while before the First World War, but the difficulties of managing five miles away from the mainland, on an island which is surrounded by the most dangerous currents in England, proved too great. So the rock was left to the gulls and the visitors from Weston-super-Mare who wanted to avoid the licensing laws, until it was once again needed as a garrison.

At the other end of Mendip, on Postlebury Hill, which for all its proximity to the town of Frome is as remote as an island, stands the more substantial ruin of a farmhouse, which was the home of John Gunthorpe, the Dean of Wells from 1471 to 1498. It was inhabited until 1906, and stands on the probable site of a Roman villa, beside a small pit (now planted with larch trees) which yielded some of the finest potting clay in the land. So this was a busy place once, but now nature is rapidly reclaiming the gaunt walls of this lost house and a tree grows in place of one of the main chimneys.

Yet it is not so sad as the seventeenth-century manor farmhouse at nearby Cloford, which is standing still, but not for long, I fear. It is used as an office and general store by a farmer content to see it decay while he lives in his modern bungalow and ruins the valley with farm buildings put up for immediate convenience, with no consideration of design or harmony with the surrounding landscape.

The silage towers and large slurry drums which are a part of modern farming can never fit easily into any landscape, but many Mendip farmers do somehow manage to combine both old and new in ways that are not so jarring. The best can adapt old buildings to suit modern needs as Mr Gay has done; and the great double stone-built barn at Doulting, where the Abbot of Glastonbury's corn was stored, is still fully used for farm purposes. It is a delight to anyone travelling along the main road going east out of Shepton Mallet. Other more remote and less historic but equally pleasing barns, like the ones which are reached by the green lane of Dursden Drove in the hills above Wells, have been well restored for farm purposes. With sometimes less happy results, some farmers in the villages have sold their barns for conversion to domestic dwellings, and used the money for more functional but less aesthetically pleasing new buildings.

"Farmers are the main protectors of the countryside," says Sir William Rees-Mogg, the former editor of *The Times*, whose family has owned land on Mendip for centuries, and who himself undertook the restoration of the eighteenth-century Ston Easton Park, the largest house in the region. Ideally, of course, he is right, the best farmers do work with nature to care for the land, which gives them their livelihood. Where that happens the farms enhance the landscape they make; its destruction comes from greed for immediate gain.

That is no new thing. John Leland complained about the early enclosures undertaken by a Mr Bampfylde in the village of Hardington near Radstock: " . . . and so now house lefte but his owne, and he pulleth doune the churche, and it is scarse known were the parsonage house stode, to which there is known to be glebe belonging but where it lyith will hardly be founde; therefore some speedy care would be had to loke to it." At least those snatched acres have in some measure gone back to the community, for Hardington is now farmed by Radstock's Independent Co-operative Society.

CHAPTER II

Fairs and Markets

SOMEHOW THE PRODUCE from the farms has to get to the markets, and that traffic draws further lines on the landscape. The case was much more extreme when livestock had to be driven many miles, but even now when they are netted down under trailers or transported in large trucks, they make quite an impact on overladen roads. Changing to bottom gear in order to follow such a cattle truck up hill, or waiting patiently as the herd goes to and from milking, hoping the accompanying bull will not decide to try his weight against a Leyland bonnet, I think of the old drovers. Men like the Easton drover, John Butt, who went from Cheddar to Wells, beneath the southern cliffs of Mendip, picking up cattle on his way.

He rode in a pony and trap, relying on his dogs to control the cattle, which had bells attached to their long horns to make other travellers aware they were coming, and to warn farmers along the route to keep their own livestock safely penned. It must have been a rowdy, smelly cavalcade, but John Butt's much-frequented route was at least safe enough. Higher up on the more lonely stretches of the hills, right up to the end of the last century, drovers could expect to be attacked by footpads.

Yet droving (the local term is "hunting") livestock to the regular markets or simply to another farm was a regular part of the week's work. For sheer tedium driving pigs must have been the worst. Walter Baber remembers how lads had to take the piglets from his father's farm to buyers ten or twelve miles away. The boys did it by filling their pockets full of pebbles, which they then threw on either side of the animals to keep them walking straight ahead. By this method you may be able to keep a young pig going in the direction you want, but there is no way you can make him move at all once he has had enough. When that happened, there was nothing the boy could do, come rain or shine, but sit about and wait for the creatures to get on to their feet again.

13

Nowadays most of the cattle from the western part of the region are sold in the Avon Livestock Centre, a hideous concrete Smithfield, which stands beside the Bristol road on the northern side of the hills. Every Tuesday, from a quarter to eight in the morning, van loads of cattle (dairy cows, store bullocks and calves) together with some sheep and a few pigs are driven up to the market. It is enough to make a non-participant turn vegetarian, at least it has me seriously questioning whether as a nation we really do need to eat meat regularly once or twice a day.

The queens of the market are the well-groomed dairy heifers who can make anything up to a thousand pounds in the auction; the most pathetic creatures there are the newly born calves, staggering into the ring to be bought up by the veal producers; the saddest are the barren cows, lumbering dirty beasts sold by the hundredweight for their meat. Still that is not the worst of it. The worst is what happens to the men who handle the animals, rushing to get their unpleasant work done, and being brutalized themselves by the way they feel they have to treat creatures, which they realize are not things, for they use their voices to control them.

Priddy Fair is a much pleasanter occasion, even if a good many of the sheep on sale there are going to end up as "lamb". At least it all takes place in the open air. Up on Priddy Green, by Manor Farm, where at weekends the cavers prepare for their underground adventures, there stands a pile of hurdles, thatched to protect them from the weather. They are a reminder of the annual sheep fair, which has been held here since 1347, when, as tradition has it, it was moved from Wells in an endeavour to check the contagion of the Black Death.

The business that is transacted at Priddy Fair is every bit as serious as that which goes on at the Avon Livestock Centre. The importance of the sheep auction that takes place here is not diluted by the fairground music and the circling of the big dipper a few yards away from the pens; nor by the crowds who flock here to see what they can pick up among the stacks of farmyard junk and old machinery of all sorts that are offered at bargain prices. For Priddy Fair is still thought of as a good day out even by those who would never venture on the swings and roundabouts. Farmers like Walter Baber, who have never gone in for sheep (he was a beef and dairy man and says that "sheep starve cows"), still think of Priddy Fair as a good way to meet their neighbours.

The sheep fair at Priddy is the sole survivor of a dozen or so Mendip village fairs that were held up to the beginning of this century, each with their dates allocated by ancient charters. It used to be held on August 21st, whatever day of the week that chanced to fall on, but this date has now been changed to a Wednesday in the second half of the month. The real business of the day is managed by King Miles & Co., a long-established firm of estate agents and surveyors, who also supply the auctioneers for the Avon Tuesday livestock market. At Priddy these men with their microphones stand up on trucks which are slowly driven past each pen. They do their work with a vocal staying power that would be the envy of most opera singers, keeping up a breakneck speed of patter and apparently never taking time off to breathe. At the same time they take note of bids so discreetly placed, that although I stood at the ringside while individual rams were being rapidly auctioned off by Philip Vennor, who comes from a farming family in the Quantocks, I never once spotted the successful bidder until his name was officially proclaimed.

Priddy is not entirely a local sale. Farmers come from as far afield as Cornwall, the Home Counties, the Midlands and East Anglia to bid for the black-faced Suffolks, the long-eared, white-faced Border Leicesters and the hardy Dorsets. Among these pens of traditional English sheep a scattering of the newly popular Jacobs and the delicate Soay are creeping in, but they have no part in the main business of the day. And although Priddy Fair was noted in the eighteenth century as a sale of oxen and horses as well as sheep, no cattle are to be seen here now. A few horses and ponies may change hands, but that is a side issue. The main purpose of the day is sheep.

Its counterpart on east Mendip, up to the middle of the nineteenth century, was the sheep fair at Mells, which used to be held on Michaelmas Monday. It came to an end because the Horner family, who have long had a tight hold on this feudal village, objected to the disturbance of the sabbath caused by the rough lot of men who came to get the fair ready. They tried changing the day to a Tuesday, but it never caught on and the fair was lost. Nobody at Priddy ever had any such scruples whatever day of the week the fair was held on, and some of the credit for its long life must go to the owners of the New Inn on the green, built only a quarter of a century after the fair started and doing very good business out of it ever since.

There is a definite distinction to be made between fairs and markets. The former are annual events, although it was always possible for a town or village to be allowed two or more fairs a year on separate charters. The latter are regular weekly or monthly "shops", frequently taking place round a market cross, like the six-sided covered crosses at Shepton Mallet and Cheddar, put up for the convenience of traders, and as a way of reminding them to be honest in their dealings.

The fortunes of the markets, like that of the fairs, went up and down with the years. In 1860, John Farbrother, local historian and headmaster of Shepton Mallet school, complained that the market in that town, which had once been one of the most important "pitched" and "ready money" markets in the locality, was showing symptoms of decay. The coming of the railways was to revive it, and by the end of the century a monthly cattle market was also established in the town. In Farbrother's time the fruit and vegetable tolls were still much the same as they had been in 1612 "ffor Apples, Pears, Carrotts, Turnips and Plumbs, two out of a Pott or Bag, or one Penny, at the election of the seller".

I cannot tell whether these rates were general in a region which, small as it is, can produce so many differences. But I do know that there was something of an uproar in February 1983, when the traders in Wells market were threatened with a hundred per cent rent rise. This market is held on Wednesdays and Saturdays, to the delight of the coach loads of summer visitors, the more discerning of whom can buy pottery glazed in the traditional Somerset manner which goes back to the sixteenth century, and some unusual culinary herbs raised on the northern edge of Mendip, at Chew Stoke. For the locals there is a travelling fish stall, a cheese van, a mobile bookshop from Castle Cary, and the chance to pick up vegetables that are much fresher and cheaper than those in the shops. You can get clothes here too. Good cheap cottons from the Indian traders; expensive white calico Victorian nightdresses from the antiques stall; and cut-price, good value things for the children. All this takes place in the open, in front of the present post office which was the covered market hall until 1835. Beside that building is the gateway of the Bishop's Eye, leading out of the market place to the moated palace by the cathedral.

It is competition from the High Street shops and chain stores which has taken most of the colour and spirit out of today's markets. Deploring the present state of the market at Radstock (a town which only attracts the most discriminating tourists), a writer in the *Somerset Guardian* of September 30th 1977 complained that nowadays it was "all packed up by lunch time". He lamented the old days when the facilities of the market included an open cart where people could have their painful teeth pulled.

Farrington Gurney, some four miles to the west of Radstock, used to have the best regular market for Mendip farmers. It was held every Monday until 1971, and in the good times of the railways, dealers took the train from Bristol to Hallowtrow and then walked the uphill mile to the market. As well as the usual livestock and farm produce on sale, buyers could find an unusual line in rabbits. They had been caught out of the stone walls around the fields, and reputedly tasted much better than the ones that burrow in the ground in the usual way.

In the eastern part of Mendip the great fairs of history were all connected with the cloth trade. The one held at Nunney under a thirteenth-century charter was briefly revived in 1959 for the purpose of raising money to re-erect the village cross in its original position by the brook, where all the business of the village had taken place for centuries.

The most important of the annual cloth fairs was held at Norton St Philip to the south of Bath. In that area the rock is of oolite limestone as it is in the Cotswolds, so the slate-roofed dwellings of the village look more like those of Gloucestershire than the Somerset edge of Avon. The houses which open on to raised cobbled pavements are dominated by the fifteenth-century George Inn where Judge Jeffreys held his summary courts after Monmouth's rebellion. Norton St Philip was a focus for the cloth fairs long before that seventeenth-century outrage, for it had a charter for its fair from 1255. Originally it was for three days in May, but so great was the pressure of business that it was extended to five days in 1353. Cattle were a subsidiary part of the fair in those days, but they continued to be sold here long after the cloth trade had left Somerset. Norton St Philip's cattle fair continued to 1902.

Cattle and horses, most especially the latter, also completely took over the fair at Binegar which formerly concentrated on cloth on the Tuesday of its four-day Whitweek fair. That fair was of fairly recent origin, having been moved up to the village from Wells in the seventeenth century, once again in an attempt to stop the spread of plague. Its importance as a horse fair grew during the nineteenth century, for until then oxen were the main working animals on Mendip farms.

The sale of horses went on at Binegar until 1955, temporarily revived after an immediate pre-war period in which people complained that it was petering out into "an assembly of gypsies", who annoyed the local farmers by trying to scrounge free grazing in the surrounding fields for the horses they hoped to sell.

Of the specialist fairs on Mendip, only the sheep at Priddy and the cheese at Frome remain. But you have to look hard to find the cheese at the late-summer Frome Cheese Fair. It is all but swamped by the varied entries and amusements of a popular agricultural show. There are classes for pedigree cattle including the beautiful shorthorns, whose hairy udders which make so much work in the ultra-hygienic routines of a modern milking parlour have caused them to be ousted by the sleeker and more productive Friesians; a show ring for thoroughbred horses where jumping and all sorts of equestrian displays take place; a florists' tent, with science fiction exotica from specialist nurseries throughout the area; an array of agricultural machinery; and a journey through time and space in a large tent which houses goats of every age and nation.

It is the cheese that takes the finding. It is housed in a tent sadly dwarfed by those given over to the other exhibits. At least it stands in the place of honour by the main gate. To an uninitiated visitor the entries can seem disappointing. Only a very few round cheeses are on show, and none are displayed in the traditional truckle cube. Like a supermarket nightmare, the immense, shining blocks of cheese await the judges who will take a small sample out of each and test it for smell, consistency, texture and flavour.

In 1982 the champion cheese of the show was a fifteen-month-old Cheddar, which earned the coveted blue sash for the Campbelltown Creamery in Argyll. Yet that was not such a humiliation for Mendip as it might appear, for the Scottish cheese makers learnt their skill from Mr Fred Akerman, a retired cheese maker from the Mendip firm of Unigate, who spends his retirement travelling as far north as the Orkneys to spread his skill. Scottish Cheddar is now a thoroughly legitimate cheese, and has been since 1871, when a Scot, Robert Porteous, steward to the great house of Marston Bigot on the outskirts of Frome, decided to model the Somerset annual Cheese Fair on the one held at Kilmarnock in his native country.

Frome Cheese Fair is a direct descendant of the town's September Fair, whose charter goes back to 1270 when William and Joan Braunch were granted the right to hold a fair at their Manor of Frome for three days, on the vigil feast and morrow of the nativity of St Mary. In 1785 this September Fair was mentioned as a cheese fair only, while the three other Frome fairs (now extinct) held in February, July and November dealt in both cattle and cheese. All the Frome fairs took place in the streets of the town, with the cheese carefully set out on straw-covered pavements before the churchyard gates.

Frome Agricultural Society was formed in 1817, and this body is responsible for the September Fair in which the cheese now plays such a minor part. That society had the same aims for its locality as the more widely based Bath and West Agricultural Improvement Society, founded in 1777, whose first public exhibition was devoted entirely to fat sheep, and which was held at the Society's Bath headquarters during its annual meeting in December 1790. Although the main aim of the Bath and West was to establish agriculture as a "science as well as an art", it was also concerned with more general social issues and championed the cause of the small children who were used to scrape the soot from the stone and brickwork of farmhouse chimneys.

Until 1965 the Bath and West used to hold its show at a different place throughout the region each year. Since that date is has made its permanent home at Evercreech just outside Shepton Mallet. The early June show that is held there now under royal patronage is really a national social event, and many of the local farmers find that they simply cannot afford the time to attend it at such a busy time of year. They much prefer the late-August, Mid-Somerset Show, which has now been running for 130 years, and which, like Frome Cheese Fair, has room for more local professional and amateur enterprises. In 1982 the Bishop of Bath and Wells won a prize for honey; while 89-year-old Mrs Mabel Ham of Cheddar, who has had exhibits at the show for the last 84 years, was a winner in the display of floral art containing the greatest number of grasses. There is still an emphasis on local crafts at this show, with the Somerset Rural Life Museum at Glastonbury arranging a demonstration of wheelwrighting, and local spinners giving visitors a chance to see them at work.

The inclusion of demonstrations of rural skills may be a matter for nostalgia now, but in the past they made a serious contribution to farming economy. When Walter Baber married and moved from his father's farm in the stone wall country of Chewton plain to the hedges of east Mendip around Evercreech, he became grateful to the competitions organized at the Mid-Somerset Show, where he learnt to become adept at the difficult craft of hedging. It is a skill that has left him with a scorn for the mechanical hedge trimmers which go along the lanes now, killing off both hedges and trees.

Like motor shows in the cities, the agricultural shows and fairs are still places where a lot of business changes hands, but throughout the ages, most of the people who go to them regard the outing as a holiday jaunt. No wonder that serious men like John Billingsley complained that such gatherings merely gave the tenant farmers an opportunity to tell lies about the landowners.

There were three fairs at Shepton Mallet in John Farbrother's time: a Waterloo Fair held on June 18th; one at Kilver Street on August 8th; and a roisterous Furmenty Fair on Easter Monday. He found them all to be "trysting places for itinerant artists of the Drama and Ballet, the Acrobat and the Conjurer, with their Satellites the Raree-show, and Turnabouts for juvenile equestrians and aeronauts". He even re-corded, with some distaste, that "Sales of so unnatural a character as knocking down your wife to the highest bidder, have, on several occasions been transacted here". The last time that happened, the "better half" was coolly handed over for a crown with a halter round her neck.

No wonder that fairs, even more than theatres, were anathema to the Puritans. In 1635 the vicar of Chew Magna put a stop to the annual St Giles Fair at Dundry by claiming back the piece of church land where it was traditionally held, on the excuse that he could not countenance the bloody sport of cudgel fighting, which all too often left the contestants with their heads split open. He had a strong case. Fighting with cudgels or single sticks was a brutal sport in which the first to draw blood from his opponent's head was the winner. Some contestants even drank gunpowder before the fight to stop the flow of blood.

Yet it was a sport that was conducted with some ceremony. The contestants used a clumsy mock foil, an ash stick fitted with a wicker-work butt to protect the hand; and in company with more aristocratic fencers they saluted each other before the start of a bout. "Keep up your butt and God preserve your eyesight" were the words they used. It was very much a favourite Somerset sport, and in 1780, at The Golden Lion in Wrington, the "men of Somerset" challenged "the rest of the world" to a cudgel fight.

These mock heroics were all part of the fun of the fair, which for a child can still be an enchanted wonderland far removed from the real business of the occasion. Mr Den Day, who was born in Banwell near the western edge of Mendip on January 1st 1899, remembers the annual cattle fair in that village. It was a fair that went on until the

1950s, but he was thinking of how it was in the days before the First World War when he wrote his reminiscences for the Banwell Society of Archaeology.

The fair was always held on the nearest Monday to January 18th, the cattle coming into the hillside village by the flat east street, which runs between Banwell and Sandford. Mr Day's father who lived at the corner of that street used to board up all his windows to prevent the cows putting their horns through them. But it was not so much the cattle that stuck in his mind as the fun and games that accompanied the sale. "All along the front of our house in the Square," he wrote, "were stalls which used to sell all kinds of articles and at night they were all lit up. At the corner of The Lane the 'Cheap Jack' used to be selling his watches. Sometimes he put half a sovereign along with one, but you were lucky to be the one to get it. The fire Station was open all day with a big fire going and the farmers used to go in and warm themselves. Snow was often about on Banwell Fair days."

CHAPTER III

Gruffy Ground: Lead, Coal and Stone

UBLEY RAKE, STANDING above the old mining lands of Charterhouse, is arguably the coldest place on Mendip. It is a bare ridge of high land, where old lead mine workings intermingle with the almost vanished ruins of the nineteenth-century manager's appropriately named Bleak House. From here you can look down on acres of "gruffy ground", that is land pock-marked by the grooves left by miners. For the wealth of Mendip lies as much in its rocks and minerals as it does in its top soil; and men's work in digging these valuable commodities out of the hills leaves more permanent marks on the landscape than agriculture ever can.

The "gruffy ground" of Mendip is far more widespread and less regular than the straight lines of Derbyshire's lead mining rakes. The term is used quite loosely for any ground on which mining operations have taken place. Strictly speaking the "gruffs" were the mine shafts, going down a hundred feet or so, lined with dry stone walling and connected by long underground galleries. As well as these there were shallow lanes, only a few feet deep and running for a hundred yards or more, where a vein of lead showed near the surface. Among the rocks of Ubley rake it is easy to trace their courses. It was in these places that the Mendip miners ("groovers") spent their working hours. Ubley also has traces of the old horse whin, where the circling animal operated a winch for the mining machinery.

All the visible remains here only date from the nineteenth century, but lead mining on Mendip was certainly going on in the Iron Age. Indeed it was probably rumours of the wealth of Mendip lead that gave the Romans the final incentive to invade this cold and clammy island.

The conclusive evidence for Roman mining on Mendip comes mainly from Charterhouse, where major excavations took place in the latter part of the nineteenth century; and from the discovery of solid, well-shaped pigs of lead, carefully date-marked, and apparently less carefully dropped on their way to export *via* Old Sarum and the ports of the south coast. These are now on display in the museums at Taunton and Wells.

On the surface the Roman mining activities at Charterhouse have been obliterated by the grooves, buddle pits and re-smelting flues of much later lead miners. Only a circular, sandy earthwork in a field on the hillside across the road from the mines is left to indicate where the amphitheatre stood. From the air it is possible to make out the traces on the land which indicate the position of a small military fort. No excavations have as yet been done on the site to prove its existence, but if the aerial photographs are found to be correct in their indications, then this place would have been the barracks of the Second Legion, whose men controlled the working of the mines, where British slaves, no doubt, did the labouring. The whole operation was managed and administered by an agent on behalf of the Emperor.

We know that a certain Ascanius was one such manager, for his name is engraved, along with other details, on one of the pigs of lead. I hope he was as happy on Mendip as those twentieth-century Italians, who came here as prisoners of war and chose to make this place their permanent home. At any rate, he would surely have enjoyed the thought that long after his legions had packed up and gone home, a replica of the Capitol Hill statue of the wolf suckling Romulus and Remus, put up by one of his latter-day fellow countrymen, should amaze travellers on the main Bristol road out of Wells.

There is only some scant evidence, found on Winterhead Hill above Shipham, to show that the Mendip lead mines were worked during the Dark Ages. But although the activity may have abated then, it would not be reasonable to conclude that it ever ceased completely, for by the early Middle Ages it was certainly flourishing and there is nothing to show that there was ever any dramatic rediscovery of ore.

The early documents recognize the wealth to be realized from the mines, and prove that the church was not slow to make its own claims sure. On November 26th 1189, Reginald, Bishop of Bath (Wells had a cathedral but no bishop at that time) received a charter from Richard I granting him the right to mine lead on Mendip. His thirteenth-century successor, Jocelyn, was given a more specific tenure. His charter (dated May 4th 1235) allowed him to start digging at Hidun in the Royal Forest of Mendip.

23

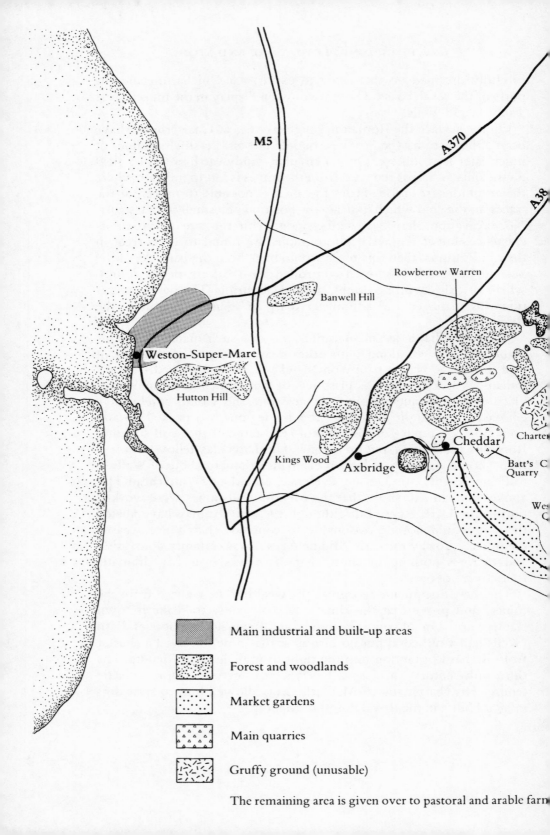

M5

A370

A38

Rowberrow Warren

Banwell Hill

Weston-Super-Mare

Hutton Hill

Kings Wood

Axbridge

Cheddar

Charter

Batt's C
Quarry

Wes
C

	Main industrial and built-up areas
	Forest and woodlands
	Market gardens
	Main quarries
	Gruffy ground (unusable)

The remaining area is given over to pastoral and arable farm

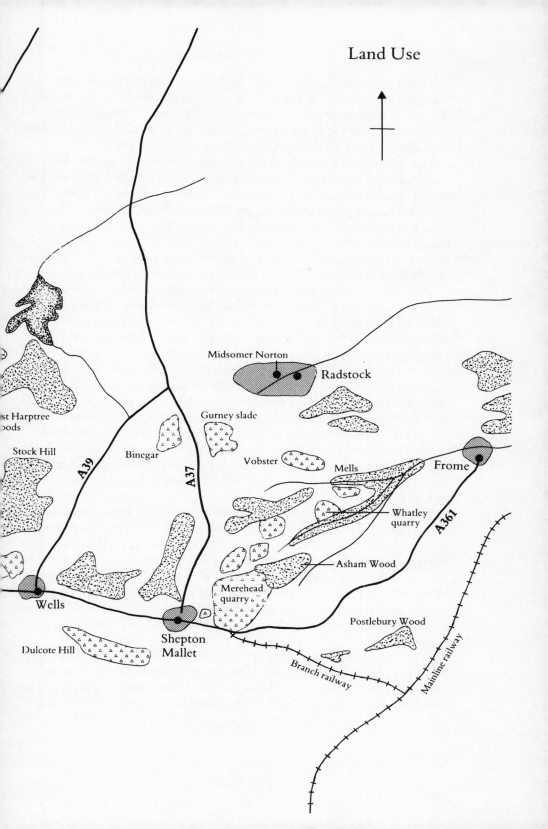

Land Use

Midsomer Norton

Radstock

Gurney slade

st Harptree
oods

Stock Hill

Binegar

Vobster

Mells

Frome

A39

A37

Whatley
quarry

A361

Asham Wood

Merehead
quarry

Postlebury Wood

Wells

Shepton
Mallet

Dulcote Hill

Branch railway

Mainline railway

That Hidun no longer exists. It became Charterhouse when the Carthusian monks of Witham Friary, to the south of Frome, obtained this extra land on Mendip, primarily as grazing ground. It was on August 28th 1283 that Edward I granted the prior and his foundation the right to work all the lead mines they could find there.

The Church did not hold an absolute monopoly of the Mendip mines, and by the sixteenth century the area was divided into four lead reeves, each subject to its own jurisdiction and administered by a spiritual or temporal lord holding his right from the monarch. The reeves or liberties were Charterhouse minery (the most westerly of the four); Priddy, which was known as St Cuthbert's and owned by the Bishop of Bath and Wells; Chewton owned by the Waldegrave family; and Harptree, which included the mines on Smitham Hill.

The actual mining was done by independent miners who worked their own stretch of land, paying lot lead (a royalty of ten per cent) either to the lord of the manor or direct to one of the four Lords Royal of Mendip. As these "tenant" miners could manage to achieve comparative wealth, there were frequent disputes, and a strict code of laws was drawn up which covered the whole area. Ten laws or customs laid down the conditions under which an individual could start working a mine on ground owned by one of the four Lords Royal. A miner was entitled to stake his claim by standing waist deep in a groove, and throwing his tools to the left and right. The distance to which he could fling them determined the amount of land he had a right to mine. He could then take his ore for smelting to whatever minery was most convenient but he had to pay tithes to the lord of the soil from which he got the ore.

The laws also laid down the responsibility that the miners had to one another. They were bound to retrieve the body of any of their fellows killed in an underground accident and give it a Christian burial. Anyone found stealing lead or lead ore to the value of 13½d had to forfeit his grooves. He payed this penalty by being literally burnt off the moor. He was forced into his house with all his tools, brushwood was then set up all round the building and fired. The man usually managed to jump clear, but he was banished from Mendip for ever.

In 1669, when lead mining on Mendip reached its peak and many more people wanted to make their fortunes from the ore, a new law had to be passed making it illegal to open mines on the highway. The other mining laws finally became obsolete in 1795 when most of

Mendip was enclosed. But even after that date, and particularly in the Shipham area, would-be miners still had to be restrained from digging up the roads.

In the seventeenth century it was in any case no longer the man-made laws but natural causes which frustrated miners intent on building their fortunes. In 1657 the Mendip miners sent a petition to Oliver Cromwell as Lord Protector of the Realm, asking him to take national action over the flooding of the Mendip mines, which was preventing them from reaching the deeper and richer veins. A century later, the agricultural reformer John Billingsley put his inventive powers to the matter, and came up with a most dramatic proposal for draining the mines. He suggested building a horizontal shaft or adit right through the hill from Compton Martin to Wookey Hole, but the scheme proved unworkable.

Joseph Glanvil, a seventeenth-century vicar of Frome, recorded how the Mendip lead was processed in his day from the crushing of the ore to its final casting. He explained in no less a learned journal than the *Philosophical Transactions of the Royal Society* that the fire in which it was smelted was "lighted with char-coal, and continued with young Oaken-gadds, blown with Bellows by Mens treading on them. And after the Fire is lighted, and the fireplace hot, they throw their Lead-Ore upon the wood, which melts down into the Furnace, and then with an Iron-Handle they take it out, and upon sand cast it into what form they please".

A little silver was found in the lead of the Charterhouse mines. It seems to have been known about since Roman times but most of our evidence for the extraction of silver in the area comes from an early fourteenth-century letter of complaint to the Bishop accusing the miners of stealing the silver, to which they were apparently not entitled. For some time after that date Priddy and Charterhouse lead had to be smelted at Wookey under strict supervision. It is very likely that Mendip silver found its way into the coinage of the realm in the seventeenth century, and is contained in those pieces which show a rose below the bust of the monarch indicating the presence of West Country silver. A hundred years later some silver was still being extracted from Mendip lead, for a Wells physician, Claver Morris, made a note in his diary for October 2nd 1720 referring to the bog near the Charterhouse *cupiloe*. That is a domed furnace for melting metal, which takes its name from the Roman process of cupellation, the production of silver. A more sophisticated processor was in use at

Charterhouse in the nineteenth century. The remains of this Pattinson refiner can now be seen on the gruffy ground as a flue going up hill from a square stone base. It was recently excavated by students on a course at the Charterhouse Field Centre, housed in the old village school, which once served the scatter of farms on this part of Mendip.

At the height of the "lead rush" many veins of lead were located by dowsers, who divined it in the same way as water is discovered, and the word "dowsing" was indeed a coinage of a Mendip man, the seventeenth-century philosopher, John Locke, born at Wrington in 1632. Billingsley later referred to the process of finding a particular substance under the earth by the movement of a forked branch held in the hands as "josing".

From the time of the Iron Age, most Mendip lead was exported, at least out of the area and frequently overseas. The Romans used it for the pipes conducting the thermal springs at Bath; and from Norman times it was used in church building. That demand went on through the centuries, and at least one document (from Axbridge in 1626) survives to prove that it was quite usual to send to "Mendeepe on Charterhouse" for lead to repair the church roof.

In the nineteenth century the mines, which had seemed to be worked out, had a brief revival when it was discovered that there was still ore to be extracted from the "slag", or refuse, left by previous generations of miners. That re-smelting process started in the Charterhouse mines in 1824, and fifteen years later it was general practice throughout Mendip. Nicholas Ennor, a Cornish mining engineer, was the brains behind this re-smelting. It was he who installed the Cornish "Buddles", circular pits lined with masonry in which the slag was prepared for smelting. A rather elaborate version of one of these can still be seen in Biddlecombe at West Horrington in the hills above Wells, and traces of others remain in the Charterhouse area, where they are visible as shallow circular depressions surrounded by fragments of stone wall. Ennor also built the horizontal flues in which the smoke, heavily charged with lead vapour, had to pass before being expelled from tall chimney stacks. There were once four of these on Mendip; one remains. Built in the Cornish style, tapering from the bottom, it stands in the middle of a forestry plantation on Smitham Hill above East Harptree. The lower two-thirds of that chimney are limestone, the upper third and cap have been restored with brick. The hill on which it stands gets its name from the mining process, for Smitham is the term for the pieces of ore allowed through the wire bottom of a sieve.

In 1860, when the Mendip Mining Company was working at Charterhouse, 20 to 25 per cent of Roman and Medieval refuse was found to be extractable lead. After the slag had been washed in pits, and stirred by a vertical paddle wheel, the slime was put into the flues to be fired, after which the pure lead condensed on the walls and roof. It was not cheaply extracted, in fact young children gave their lives for it. For often it was the orphans from the Cheddar poor house who had the task of chipping the poisonous lead, made all the more lethal by an admixture of arsenic, out of the flues. It can have been of little consequence to those boys and girls that, in 1865, the Charterhouse workings yielded 326½ tons of lead and 1300 ounces of silver. For it was not until 1876 that they were protected from such exploitation by the law forbidding the employment of children under ten.

Soon after that lead mining on Mendip came to an end. By 1880 St Cuthbert's mine on Priddy was the only one left working, and about 50 men were employed there. It closed in 1908. Both there and at Charterhouse, mounds of worked-out slag, black and shining, stand as a memorial to an industry, as cruel as most. They stand between the flues grown romantic in ruin, and lovingly preserved and reconstructed by members of the Mendip Society, and the once lead-poisoned water where the refuse was washed. Sea campion grows boldly here, and in summer the adders, grass snakes and slow-worms slide across the paths among the gruffy ground.

Not all nineteenth-century lead mining was a matter of reprocessing. In some areas the old tradition of independent mining for fresh ore persisted. Frank Knight, who wrote about the west of Mendip in the first decades of this century, recounts that mining was carried out around Winscombe "within living memory", and that it was rumoured that some of the galleries extended as far as Winterhead Hill a couple of miles away. Although no mines had been worked at Winterhead since about 1850, Knight could report that in his day the site of the pit was still pointed out "from which the grandfather of the village blacksmith took out by candle-light, five pounds' worth of ore".

Lead mining never went on without disputes of one kind or another. Even though hardly any of the mines were worked by individuals during the nineteenth century, there was often trouble between men and management, and between the mines and other concerns on the hills. In the 1870s the average wage was twelve shillings a week, and all pay tickets from the Charterhouse works carried a printed warning to the effect that the captain of the lead mines could fine any man a week's wages if the work was not properly done. Sometimes he had to go to court to prove his case; but it was not that issue which brought Joseph Filer and Mark Brunt before the Wrington magistrates on Monday January 6th 1873, although they were eventually both fined and fired. Their crime was not only to lazily throw away quantities of metal during the washing process, but to threaten to throw the "gaffer" into the pond too, when he found fault with them.

More serious disputes arose out of the pollution of the local water supplies by the lead from the mines. In 1861, the case was heard in Wells assizes, with much bitterness on both sides, between Nicholas Ennor (by then the proprietor of St Cuthbert's mine at Priddy) and the Hodgkinson family, who owned the paper mill at Wookey, and who claimed that their water source had been severely contaminated by the lead. Yet it is the farmers, not the paper-makers, who have suffered most directly from any pollution caused by lead mining; and even without that hazard, the bitter divide between the solid, settled hard-working farmers, struggling with a harsh, cold land, and the carefree, get-rich-quick groovers was inevitable. That rivalry for the wealth of the hills is explored in Walter Raymond's Hardyesque novel *Two Men o' Mendip*, in which the groover hero, Gyles Standerwick, finally marries a Charterhouse farmer's daughter and turns farmer himself. There are good precedents in real life for that, but more often it was the farmer who turned groover when he discovered a seam of lead in his land.

In 1543 William Reynes of Chew made a will describing himself as a husbandman, although his bequests included a hundredweight of lead apiece to the churches of Blagdon and Compton Martin. His was not an isolated case, although that dual source of wealth was not available to the tenant farmers once the land was enclosed. Any lead found in their fields was immediately claimed by the landlord.

That was a comparatively small frustration compared to "minedering" — the destruction of cattle and crops caused by lead in the soil — which a few Mendip farmers still have to contend with. The best of them do it by assiduously learning to farm this difficult land, relying on the wisdom and experience of their predecessors as well as on the advice of specialists from the Ministry of Agriculture and the veterinary college at Langford, where a special study of the effects of the lead in the soil is still being carried out.

Mr Bill Young, who farmed Lower Farm, Charterhouse in the 1920s, knew that it was wrong to plough too deeply and stir up the lead. Pastoral farmers have followed the example of the medieval Carthusian monks of Witham, who only grazed sheep on their hilltop holdings. For some reason, sheep, moles, rabbits and cats are not affected by the lead, which builds up in the liver and kidneys of cattle. There it stays, seeming to do no harm until it is suddenly released into the brain and the creature goes mad. Blind and frothing at the mouth, the animal is usually dead within six hours.

Lead poisoning is only a matter of soil contamination. It cannot get into the fibres of growing grass, and it is not soluble in water; but it is impossible to prevent the earth's dust from getting on to grazing land in dry weather (and there can be enough lead in a mole hill to kill four cows), or to stop cattle drinking muddy water lead and all. This danger has always been known and the Minery Court held in Chewton Mendip in 1573 forbade the "Buddling" or washing of ore during the summer months when cattle grazed on the hills.

Now that all farms are on piped water, there is no threat of pollution through the water supply. Yet in times of exceptional flooding such as that of 1968, the lead from the topsoil can get washed into ponds and streams miles from the site of the mines, and kill all the life in them.

Lead is poison to men as well as to animals, a fact that was appreciated at least from the seventeenth century. By that date it was accepted that work in the mines led to an early death, and that for some reason, which we now know to be due to lead in the brain, violence and lawlessness were greater among lead miners than any other working group. In fact it was so bad that in 1607 a law was passed forbidding any further mining licences on Mendip. Still the connection between lead and poison was not fully made. Miners still used water from the mines when they prepared their food, a proceeding made all the more hazardous by the traces of arsenic in the soil.

Lead has been the most exploited, but it is by no means the only mineral to have been condensed from the steam pushed up through the volcanic rocks of Mendip. In the 1790s a calamine of remarkably pure quality was found at Mells to the east of the region, far away from the main lead mining area. However it was at Shipham to the west of Charterhouse that calamine was most fully exploited. In Chapter Seven I shall explore the effect those mines had, and are still having, on the history of that village and the people who live there.

The hills also contained a rare oxychloride of lead. It was given the name of Mendipite in 1823 by the Swedish chemist, J. J. Berzelino, who found it among a collection of minerals in Stockholm. It has mainly been found around Dolebury and at the head of Ebbor Gorge, although I have heard of a piece being discovered at Long Wood by Cheddar Gorge.

Mendipite is by no means the end of the story. In 1960, a survey was done of the whole mineral wealth of the area. With admirable restraint the company which undertook this work refrained from publishing their findings. Rare minerals lie under Mendip hills, but the mining of them could seriously threaten Bristol's water supply, and would certainly destroy the landscape.

The Mendip hills change their character at Wells. This is true for the whole nature of the landscape, and it is also true of the mineral wealth that lies beneath the hills. To the west of the city is the gruffy ground of the lead mines, to the east are the shapely batches of the now defunct coal mines.

The division is not completely clear cut. A survey of 1571 showed that lead was once mined in small quantities at the village of Kilmersdon, on the outskirts of Radstock. But before that, at least from 1437 when it was first recorded, the main mining in this grey stone valley village was for coal. As with the lead at Charterhouse, the mining of the coal around Kilmersdon was mostly an individual matter; the "colepytts" being worked by the tenants who farmed the land.

Coal was also worked in the Mells area at that time. Apart from legal documents, the first reference to Somerset coal comes from one of John Leland's reports of his visit to the county in 1545. "There cometh a brook from the coal pits of Mendip, and striketh by south into the bottom of Mells, and then runneth in Frome river," he wrote. Michael Drayton in his *Polyolbion* of 1612 turned this into verse:

> . . . and Frome to her disgrace
> Since scarcely ever washt the coalflek from her face.

By the end of the 1670s, coal was being mined at Farrington Gurney, Midsomer Norton and Paulton, and a few years later the Bristol and Somerset coalfields were producing 100,000 tons per annum. At the beginning of the next century, the Wells physician, Claver Morris, noted in his diary that the cost of coal was £1 a ton in the city, and ten shillings at the pithead. Small wonder, then, that farmers from as far west as Shipham for many years sent carts twenty miles or more to collect their coal.

The Reverend John Collinson, vicar of Long Ashton, whose history of Somerset was published in 1792, became quite lyrical on the subject of the county's excellent coals, "the veins of which are generally covered with a stony stratum, which the miners call *wark*. It splits like slate, and abounds with the impressions of fern and other plants. . . . The coal is often tinged with sulphur. Some years since one stratum wrought here was so thoroughly impregnated with it, that in all its joints it seemed to be covered with leaf-gold". He also noted that in another place nearly three hundredweight of good lead ore was found "growing to a vein of coal".

John Billingsley made a sharp distinction between the collieries to the north of Midsomer Norton, around Paulton and Camerton, supplying a high-grade coal for fivepence a bushel, most of which was sent to Bath; and those to the south of the town, from which a poorer-grade coal, at 3¾d a bushel, was produced. Some of this went to Wales *via* Portishead, where it was much in demand for lime burning. Billingsley was as tough on the miners as he was on farm labourers, asserting that their wage was "sufficiently adequate to procure them a comfortable subsistence" and complaining that a poor levy should be raised "where the wages of a collier and his family, not exceeding five persons, have been 25s per week, and their improvidence has been such, that one week's illness has brought them to the parish for assistance".

At that time, whoever found coal on his land and had the means to work it could lay claim to it. Not only did the big landowners, like the Waldegraves, lay claim to any mines their tenant farmers discovered on the land, and up to the last World War, but the haulage of coals could be part of the tenancy agreement. On Sir William Rees-Mogg's farm at Timsbury, the tenant farmer is still discovering shafts of old mines, for which the National Coal Board now has to take responsibility.

At Buckland Dinham, in a field belonging to Barrow Hill Farm, a single chimney stands in a piece of land, whose shafts are securely fenced off from the cattle who graze the kale around it. This brick tower, whose furnace worked the steam engine which lowered the men into the mines and raised the coal, is the sole visible reminder of the days, not so very long ago, when men trudged to work along Colliers Lane.

Most of those men would be walking north from Mells, where coal
has been mined since the reign of Charles II, when it was mentioned as
being among those places in "the forest of Mendipp where coal pits
are". At that time there were open cast pits at Lower Vobster to the
west of the village.

It was not until 1763 that coal was found at Radstock, but by the
time the mines were finally closed in the 1970s, that town with its
rival, Midsomer Norton, had become the centre of the Somerset coal
mines. Ray Inchley, who now delivers the mails in Radstock,
Kilmersdon and the neighbouring village of Faulkland was a N.U.M.
branch secretary for fifteen years at the Writhlington colliery on Lord
Hylton's land. He has no regrets for his 22 years in the mines,
although, in common with most miners, his father was saddened
when his two sons chose to earn their living underground.

Ray admits that it was a hard and difficult life, but the experience of
working with skilled men in such circumstances was something that
he still treasures. "It's a different world down there," he says, "you
very rarely hear people get angry with each other." Constantly living
with danger, miners have to be realists, and it is that quality together
with the precision it brings that he particularly values. He has found
that "miners are great thinkers, they have to be" for "even with the
most modern machinery, skill and extraordinary care are needed for
their work". Yet although he is grateful for his years as a miner, Ray
feels no bitterness about the closure of the Somerset pits. In his
opinion the Arthur Scargills do not reflect the views of the men who
are actually working at the coal face. They know when a pit is losing
money: "There's no taste to nothing." Yet his opinions do not block
his sympathies with the older miners who have to put up with the
stigma of unemployment, which redundancy pay cannot erase.

This does not mean that Somerset men were always keen to work
underground. Many miners' sons were able to find work on the farms
or to leave the area altogether. So in the 1950s and '60s, men from
Durham and Scotland came south to work in Radstock and Midsomer
Norton, where they joined the Italians and Hungarians who had
already started working in the Somerset mines. Many of these people
stayed on in the area after the pits closed.

The ranks of houses in which the miners lived, like the terrace on
Radstock's northern slope where Ray Inchley still has his home, were
mostly built by the pit owners. In other places, like the old mining
town of Pensford, on the Wells to Bristol road, the eighteenth-century

miners' cottages have been attractively gentrified and sold to city commuters. When the miners lived there, they would have expected to have had a communal yard with wash houses, bake houses, privvies and enough land behind those outbuildings to grow a few vegetables. That is how it was around Radstock in the early years of this century. The kitchens in which the families did most of their living were dominated by a white wood table, which was covered in between meals by a red plush cloth. The floor was grey stone slag, which might sometimes have a piece of Italian mosaic in it. Whether it did or not it was always carefully polished.

Janet Tanner's father and grandfather lived in such a house. She is a writer of popular romances, who lives in a new estate by the canalized River Somer in Midsomer Norton. When she turned her attention near to home and produced the highly successful *Black Mountain* in 1981, she based her novel on the mining tales her family had told her. And she knew something about coal mining at first hand, for when she left school in 1960 she had a job in the offices of the National Coal Board. At that time there were still six pits working.

Ted of the *Black Mountain* is an imaginative reconstruction of the real Gerald Young, who was born in 1896, and who passed his Labour Examinations at the age of twelve. That meant that he was allowed to leave school and start work underground as a carting boy, going barefoot and shirtless in the pits and pulling cartloads of coal to which he was harnessed by the cruel "gus and crook".

This seems to have been a distinctly Somerset device. It has been carefully described by A. J. Parfitt, who also went down the pits at the age of twelve. The year was 1893. "The guss is a kind of harness," he wrote in his book *My Life as a Somerset Miner*, which was published from the Miners' Office in Radstock in 1930, "it consists of a piece of one-inch rope, four feet in length. The rope had to be spliced . . . to form a girdle with a piece of chain attached called a tugger." The carting boys were expected to make this harness for themselves. A. J. Parfitt went on to tell of his first day's carting: "Then with this rope girdle around my naked waist, I was given a crook, and with the tugger through my legs I had to attach myself to a putt." The putt was a shallow box mounted on iron runners like a small toboggan.

In that manner Mrs Tanner's father carted for her grandfather, and it was usual for this to be a family matter. A miner without a carter was useless to the pit owners, and the young men who wanted to leave Somerset for the easier mines of South Wales were told that they would have to take their fathers with them. Yet many did cross the Severn Sea, and as well as their fathers they took their cheese. Caerphilly has a Welsh name, but it is a Somerset cheese, made by the same process as Cheddar but taking less than the usual six months to ripen. The miners' cogknockers (bread and cheese) was an important part of their working lives, as farmers like Robert Hodges of Crowfield Farm, Easton, fully appreciated. He was producing quantities of Caerphilly for South Wales at the turn of the century.

The main reason why Somerset miners looked for work away from home was the nature of the coal itself. The mines at the south-eastern edge of Mendip produced a very good-quality coal, but the seams are laid in twisted veins, not much more than a foot thick, folding back on themselves and overlapping at sites of geological faults. The positive aspect of this difficulty was that at least during the latter years there were relatively few accidents in the Somerset mines. Because the seams were so hard to work, everything had to be done particularly carefully and the miners came to know the pits like the backs of their hands. The greatest danger came from the fast-moving tubs of coal, whose rush down an incline was signalled by bells, which sometimes failed to give the carting boys sufficient warning.

The other threat to life and safety came from the underground water. The pumps had to be worked each night and sometimes during the day as well. On the credit side there was no danger from gases, and the explosions, such as the one that occurred at Norton Hill in 1910, were caused by dust. Mining is never completely safe, and at any time there was the possibility of a vertical rock, or a petrified tree weighing a ton or more, becoming dislodged as the coal which had supported it was removed.

Even when his work underground is long over, a miner's life can remain at risk. The deaths of all former Somerset miners still have to be reported to the National Coal Board, which has to assess whether life was shortened by pneumoconiosis. That provision is about all that is left now of Mendip's coal mining days.

The small collieries started to close down when their owners found that they could not afford to comply with the law which demands that each mine should have two air vent shafts. Edford colliery at Holcombe went in 1916, and its neighbour, Newbury at Coleford, closed in 1927. They are both now occupied by stone and concrete works.

The more profitable mines were still in full production between the wars, when the Ordnance Survey map for Radstock marked pits rather than houses. At that time the mines were all still in private ownership; it was the post-war National Coal Board which had to take the final decision to end Somerset mining. The last pit closed in the 1970s, and Ray Inchley believes that on the whole things are better in Radstock now that the mines have gone.

There is still coal here, however, in fact there is said to be eleven million tons of it lying in the ground under Ammerdown Park alone. It will probably be allowed to stay there. Nowadays it is stone that is being torn away from these hills.

In an area where rock is immediately available, quarrying of some sort has gone on as long as men have built houses. Right up to the early nineteenth century most of the ground from which the rock was removed to build farms and cottages was subsequently relevelled. At that time the quarries depended on a large labour force. In 1830 Pigot & Co.'s *National Commercial Directory* observed with some complacency of the village of Chew Magna: "Some quarries of red ochre in the vicinity, furnish a great proportion of the labouring class here with employment."

The stone getters worked in gangs of two to four men, each gang being responsible for its own surface rock. This involved blasting out the stone and breaking it up; an experienced man could crack up to 40 tons of limestone a day. It then had to be hauled away from the quarries in horse-drawn waggons, until 1896, when the Red Flag Act was repealed and steam locomotives could use the highways unimpeded by a man walking in front of them to proclaim danger.

Blasting was done by packing black grain powder, dampened so as to produce a slow burning rate, into wheat straw. Each quarry man had to contribute to the cost of the explosives used by his gang, as well as providing his own tools. The main explosive came from powder mills powered by Mendip water, and the Mendip stone it dislodged went into industrial, farm and domestic buildings. The Avonmouth docks were built out of the quarries at Sandford, and when the railways came the stations along the Cheddar Valley line were all built of Mendip dolomitic conglomerate.

Mendip churches have also been hewn out of the hills. In the thirteenth century it was the quarry at Doulting, with its mellow gold stone, that provided the building material for Wells Cathedral. Now known as St Andrew's quarry, the medieval scar on Doulting's plateau is a pleasantly romantic place to walk in, especially on a winter afternoon when there is no risk of being entangled in the undergrowth and the steep quarried cliffs are decorated with the ever-present hart's tongue fern.

Like every other quarry on Mendip, St Andrew's has been the subject of dispute. There were some fairly sharp negotiations when the monks of Glastonbury, who were the rightful owners, sold both stone and quarrying rights to the Dean and Chapter of Wells. In 1362, the Glastonbury monks were negotiating again when they made provision for stone to be quarried for Bath Abbey, to the north of the place where the Wells men had been working.

From the time of the eighteenth-century enclosures, the quarries also undertook lime burning for agricultural use, gradually taking over the processes that had been carried out on the farms, although the farm kilns remained in existence for centuries. Yet during the First World War, farmers from the village of Westbury-sub-Mendip took carts to collect lime from Underwood quarry near Wells, and so travelled five miles each way rather than use one of the limekilns in the village. On the eastern end of Mendip, the lime from Limekiln Hill at Vobster Cross just outside Mells was always much sought after; and at Francis Flower's quarry at Gurney Slade, the kiln in which lime was burnt since 1873 was in use for just over a hundred years. When that stone quarry stopped lime burning in the late 1970s the process ceased on Mendip. Now the nearest lime burning is in Derbyshire.

In other respects the devastation wrought by the Mendip quarries in these hills is as serious as that five-mile scar which I.C.I. has drawn across the White Peak in the hills round Buxton. Since the war there has been some county council control over the extension of the Somerset quarries. The present plan is to refuse quarrying permission on the hills to the west of Wells, which have been declared an Area of Outstanding Natural Beauty; and to let the stone taking go on unimpeded in the area between Shepton Mallet and Frome. In effect this means that quarrying still goes on in the west, as there is never enough money to buy the companies off. It is however harder for them to extend their works. So the Amalgamated Road Stone Company and the English China Clay company contrive to quarry Batt's Combe and Callow Hill respectively, and are likely to do so for the next twenty years.

One of the few quarries in the west which has been recently closed is the County Council's own Underwood quarry. The remaining quarries are now mainly in the hands of large consortiums; the only private family quarry on Mendip belongs to Foster Yeoman, and operates east of Wells. Its concerns are not confined to Mendip for it has operations at Botley in Hampshire and Theale near Reading, run in conjunction with its main quarry near Shepton Mallet.

The company started in 1922 when Foster Yeoman, the son of a West Hartlepool shipowner, came south and turned quarryman, with the laudable aim of reducing the unemployment rate in Somerset. He managed to find work for a hundred men. In 1983 the quarries he started were employing three hundred people, many of Foster Yeoman's employees being local farmers' sons.

The founder of the business died in 1949, and his son John, whose own two sons have since entered the business, took over the firm. By 1960 the company's main quarry and railhead were established at Merehead near Shepton Mallet, on a site that has been worked since 1920. The quarry that Foster Yeoman originally started at Dulcote on the outskirts of Wells is now mainly used for training purposes, although twenty of the firm's older men work there, producing about a thousand tons of crushed rock each day, as well as retrieving some of the ornamental agates. These are polished and sold off to the tourist shops or embodied into pieces of executive office furniture for show in the quarry's administrative block.

The destruction of Dulcote hill is a sideline to the really serious business of carting away Mendip limestone. Anyone who has the chance to look at the great electric pestle and mortar in operation will not find it too fanciful to foresee the day when Mendip becomes another lake-dotted plain. Lorry load after lorry load is tipped into this greedy monster, which smooths out the substance of the hills as though it were fruit for a purée. The stone-crushing process is a horrifying, hypnotizing example of technology at work. The only time when the rock actually challenges the strength and ingenuity of men is when there is a sudden power cut. Then the machine stops, and all the rock in the "sieve" must be manhandled out of it, a formidable task but insignificant compared to what was done when the stone was broken by hand.

In 1976, when the Somerset quarries employed about three thousand people, the hills were being removed at the rate of ten million tons a year. No further calculations have yet been published, when they are they are bound to show an increase in the rate of destruction. Modern techniques could obliterate the hills in a few generations.

To make stone quarrying pay it has to be done on a vast scale; for although roadstone is such a necessary commodity and although Mendip is the nearest available rock for the busy roads of the south-east, its cost in 1982 stood at only £2.50 a ton. So Foster Yeoman has to keep its crusher going and regularly blast away at the hills, being glad of the Home Counties connection, and grateful too for the fact that it is Mendip limestone rather than Lincolnshire jurassic that is being delivered to Suffolk three times a week. For it is roads that eat up limestone now, and if the recession had not curtailed the national road-building programme, there is no doubt that the hills would be disappearing at an even faster rate.

It seems fair enough when it was purely a local matter. Until the nineteenth century the roads were the responsibility of the local councils, and most parishes had their own quarries for that purpose. It is even just that Mendip limestone should have been used to build the section of the M5 which runs through the hills from Bristol to Bridgwater. But it is difficult to accept the destruction of the hills to supply roads for most of Britain.

Apart from the destruction of the landscape, the human cost of large-scale quarrying in terms of pollution is enormous. The Alkaline Inspectorate works closely with the quarry owners to try to minimize pollution, and new crushing machinery is always designed with the prevention of dust in mind. Yet still the fine white powder is everywhere, choking hedges and streams. The publican who runs The Bear beside the quarry at Holwell tries his best to ignore it, bravely setting out tables and sun umbrellas in his dust-laden garden. He even attracts quite a lively custom, although I have never seen anybody actually drinking outside. In fact the inn is almost an extension of its neighbouring quarry, and in the 1870s it was actually a centre for lime burning as well as for retailing beer. Even if, as one quarry official observed to me rather cynically, farmers should now be grateful for the free lime which the dust supplies, few people are prepared to be so tolerant of the nuisance the quarries cause.

At least the pollution that goes on above ground can be seen and reckoned with. Far more dangerous is the unseen disturbance that quarrying makes to the course of Mendip's many underground rivers, as rock is removed from beneath the water table. That method of deep quarrying may do something to prevent the lateral spread of the gashes in the hillsides, but it has serious implications for the flow of the water supply; and its only logical outcome is the creation of a chain of lakes in place of the hills. Some people pretend to make a virtue of that necessity.

Meanwhile the 1981 Minerals Act insists on disused workings being properly landscaped; or at least camouflaged by trees and earthworks so that visiting motorists cannot see what havoc lies behind the backdrop of landscape beside the roads. Yet some quarrying scars cannot be so easily hidden. The straight cut through Milton Hill above Wells, which was made by Italian prisoners of war working at Underwood quarry, can never been healed.

The quarries are the greatest threat to the Mendip landscape. The people who live on the surface of the hills and those who make their money out of their very substance have always been at odds, and the rivalries and disputes that used to take place between the settled farmers and the free-lancing groovers has now been replaced by the opposing interests of the quarry owners and the conservationists.

There are only two ameliorating factors. One is the present tendency for the quarries to employ professional landscape architects, who will at least plant the finished workings with trees that are native to this part of Somerset. The other is Foster Yeoman's achievement of transporting the crushed stone by rail. The Merehead quarry is linked to the eastern section of the old Cheddar Valley line, which joins the main British Rail system at Witham. Traffic congestion and pollution would certainly be a lot worse if the minor Somerset roads had to contend with several thousand lorries coming out of that one quarry alone.

CHAPTER IV

Water Power: Mendip Mills

THE MAN FROM the Bristol Waterworks lived in Twerton, once a village, now a busy suburb of Bath. His work had brought him to a remote valley bottom in eastern Mendip and there he stood with his mate, a large bunch of snowdrops in one hand, puzzling over the people who had once worked at the ruined mill fed by St Dunstan's well, whose flow it was his duty to measure. The snowdrops were everywhere, survivors of lost cottage gardens and the formal grounds of the Chichesters' house, which was demolished in 1928. Now they carpet the woods whose undergrowth hides the few remaining traces of Stoke Bottom village where the mill workers lived. At one time that mill was the property of John Billingsley who, preferring agriculture to industry, "declined that business" and sold it through an advertisement in the *Bristol Journal* of July 31st 1784.

It is only possible to explore this lost village of eastern Mendip in winter or early spring, before the tangle of brambles and tall nettles make it impossible to follow the course of the main street or trace out the few remaining walls of the forty cottages which once housed some two hundred people. Not all of them were mill workers, for up to 1841, Joseph Down, a publican, and Martha Bryant, an eighty-year-old knitter, were among the inhabitants.

In high summer when the wood is virtually impenetrable, you can still walk past the rushing diverted waters that fed two mills until work stopped in 1838; and you can go up the grassy hillside to the well, a spring which bounds out of the rock. It is a beautiful place whose romance is only just held in check by a small waterworks' enclosure. Below it, the old road, now a green track round the side of the hill, leads to the site of Billingsley's house at Ashwick Grove.

As soon as Mendip water comes out of the hills it is put to use, and for centuries, here and elsewhere, that use was the powering of water mills. In later years, many of these mills, like the one at Stoke Bottom, were engaged in making paper.

Over to the west is the village of Banwell, with its large, smooth bowling green filling the space of the pond, which was once the main source of water for the village, and the supply of power to its mills. In 1870 John Rutter found it to be "a large sheet of water in the middle of the village, with a graceful weeping willow on an island in the centre and a pair of handsome swans which form a pleasing object from the street". By 1906 things had declined. The vicar was complaining in his parish magazine that the swans formed "the only pleasing object there, for usually there is more weed than water to be seen. This condition of things is not only unsightly but is a distinct menace to the health of the village, for the pond through the pump supplies a large proportion of the population". Twenty years later the pond was filled in, and the stream that fed it diverted to reinforce Weston-super-Mare's water supply.

The public footpath, which skirts two sides of the bowling green that has taken the place of the pond, goes along the top of the old dam, through which the release of water, that drove the three mills in the centre of Banwell in the early eighteenth century, was controlled. By the 1830s there were only two mills at the dam head, one a grist mill and the other a large paper manufactory. The paper mill was established in 1710 and ran until 1850, producing a very high-quality paper, some of which was used for banknotes. In 1902 the old mill was converted into a brewery which ran until 1909, when the spring was sold to the Bristol waterworks. This caused such a local upheaval that the vicar went to London to protest at this infringement of Banwell's most jealously guarded possession.

The Emerys' mill at Banwell was only one of many paper mills throughout western Mendip. Further east the power was provided by the Axe as it flows out of the Wookey Hole caves. Two of these paper mills are still working. One is a commercial undertaking. The other, which still produces hand-made paper, mainly serves as an additional attraction to the visitors to the caves, who walk to the mill alongside the leat, lined with slabs of lias, which carries the water to power the wheel. This mill was once the biggest in Europe, producing 35,000 sheets of paper a week. Cyril Finn, who has served the paper maker's seven-year apprenticeship, now plies his craft under the watchful eyes of a stream of visitors, delighted by his rhythmic skill as he sieves the pulp and shakes it into shape in the mould to produce some five hundred sheets of paper a day. One hundred sheets go to make a post, a stack of unfinished sheets which are finally processed in a Victorian hydraulic press.

The Axe has powered a paper mill at Wookey since 1610. In 1728, the overshot mill (one in which water is forced over the wheel) was offered for sale as part of the Wookey Hole estate, together with a small grist mill. They both carried the recommendation that they never lacked water to drive them even in the hottest summer. In 1852 the mill was acquired by William Samuel Hodgkinson, and it was his descendants who eventually opened the Wookey caves to the public.

When the mill at Wookey Hole finally ceased commercial production in 1972, the St Cuthbert's mill, to the south of it, which depends on the same water supply, became the sole surviving paper mill on Mendip, although at one time the Axe alone powered five of them. Now it is in the hands of an American company which owns other mills in Dorset and Scotland. Its Somerset mill employs 146 people.

The other paper mills in the county are a matter of industrial archaeology. The remains of the one at Dulcote are clearly visible from the road going from Wells to Shepton Mallet. The redbrick Georgian mill house, with its tall chimney that was burnt down in 1904, is a private residence now. It is a pleasant place, but the wide pastoral valley of its setting cannot compete with the place where a mill once stood at Rickford, near Blagdon on the other side of the hills. A mill was here at the time of Domesday, but now the waters that powered it support a thriving colony of watercress, and the soft yellow monkey musk are nourished on its banks.

On Mendip, as elsewhere, mills, powered by water or wind, were first used for grinding corn, one of the earliest advances of technology being to mechanize the processes of pestles and mortars. The ruins of many of the Domesday corn mills, which were later converted to other uses, were still visible up to the end of the last century. One such was the mill at Moreton, turned into a gunpowder mill in 1799, and now lying under the waters of Chew Valley Lake.

Maxmill, near Winscombe, is the old mill that attracted most attention from local historians at the turn of the century. It stands at the point where several of the most ancient tracks across the hills converge. In 1892, Theodore Compton believed he had found the ruins of this old mill in the valley to the south of the village, identifying the mill dam supplied by two powerful springs; but the whole complex could have belonged to one or both of the two mills which Collinson noted in 1791 as being turned by the brook that runs through the valley between Winscombe and Banwell.

Western
Mendip:
Burrington
Combe and
Blackdown

Aspects of Mendip
farming. *Above:*
Strawberry pickers *circa*
1905. *Left:* The Model
Farm at East Harptree

Aspects of Mendip farming. *Above:* Priddy Sheep Fair. The pile of hurdles stands permanently on the village green, a reminder of this historic annual event. *Below:* A wild bee wall at Lower Farm, Charterhouse. The holes are left to encourage the bees to make honey here.

Above: St Andrew's Quarry, Doulting which provided the stone for Wells Cathedral in the twelfth century. *Below:* At the new quarry beside it a crane prepares to lift blocks of the pale gold limestone.

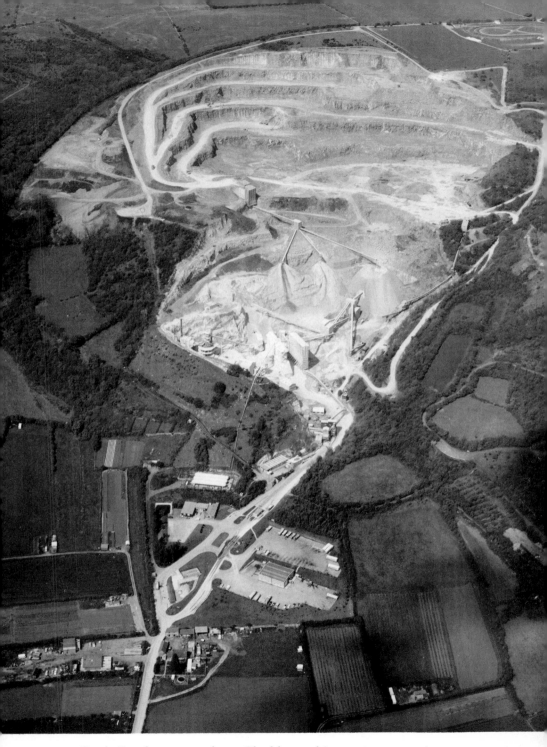

Batt's Combe quarry, above Cheddar, making as great a scar in
the hills as the natural gorge

Gruffy
Ground:
Ubley Rake at
Charterhouse

Writhlington
Colliery near
Radstock, in
1968

The ruins of Fussell's iron works at Mells. These hammer sheds once supported a three-storey building.

Frank Knight was more certain that the ivy-clad fragment which he was familiar with in Winscombe in the early years of this century was the mill recorded in Domesday. He reported that in the 1870s, the main part of that mill, roofed with thatch, was used as a cowshed, and that the water wheel was still about. Not a vestige remains today.

Being in the centre of one of the great cloth areas of England, the Mendip mills were soon put to the service of the clothiers, and to the allied processes of fulling and dyeing. The leats and millponds associated with these mills are still easily discernible in many places, although most of the buildings have disappeared.

John Billingsley's mill at Stoke Bottom was used in the process of logwood dyeing before it was converted to the production of paper. The logwood, which was composed of the heart of trees much like our whitethorns, was shipped to Bristol from Jamaica from the early eighteenth century. The logs were chopped up into splinters which were then fermented in water, at which stage they formed shiny green crystals, which produced a strong black dye.

At that time woad was still being cultivated to the north of Mendip, in the Keynsham area between Bath and Bristol. Two hundred years earlier, clothiers at Mells were mentioning woad vats in their wills, and in the eighteenth century one Harvey the Woadman of that village used a horse engine to grind the dye. They said that the woad industry at Mells died with his death; but in 1801, when the Reverend Richard Warner took an excursion to Mells from Bristol, he found workers "as deeply tinged as Ancient Britons" with the dye. Perhaps that was an indication that our remote ancestors were simply work-stained and not adorned for battle.

Fulling mills were of a much earlier date. Water power was used for that purpose in the Wells area from the thirteenth century; and in 1540, when Leland visited "the pretty market townlet", which was to become the mining village of Pensford, he found the River Chew powering several fulling mills. All that remains of that industry now are the ruins of the mill behind the Rising Sun Inn, and that probably only survives because when the cloth trade had finished, it reverted for a time to a grist mill.

It was in the south-east of the Mendip area, and particularly in and around the towns of Shepton Mallet and Frome, that the woollen mills were busiest. Michael McGarvie, Frome's leading local historian, quotes a 1721 World Atlas in which the town is mentioned as being "famous for the manufacture of broad and narrow woollen-cloths, in which it employs thousands of the poor, both old and young, so that girls of seven or eight years of age are able to earn half a crown per week in a good time of trade".

Full employment did not make for peace and content. In 1726 the Frome weavers rioted against their pay and conditions, and order was not restored until the ringleaders were clapped into Ilchester jail, and the Dragoons were stationed in the town. Yet English cloth was still in great demand, and the clothiers could not produce it fast enough. In August 1743, Lady Hertford wrote to her son Lord Beauchamp that "they cannot at this time in Wiltshire, Somersetshire and all the Western counties get labourers to bring in the harvest because all the poor people are employed by the clothiers". In 1788, the Sheppards, who were to become the wealthiest of all the Frome clothiers, established their mill, which still stands at Spring Gardens to the north of the town. Two years later Billingsley reported that a third of the seventeen hundred families in Frome were employed in the woollen industry.

By the nineteenth century it was no longer only the wool from Mendip sheep that was being turned into cloth in the mills around Frome and Shepton Mallet. By 1805 Sheppards were using Spanish and German wool at Spring Gardens; and in Shepton Mallet there was only one small woollen mill at work in the town by 1838, the rest were given over to velvet and silk. In the undergrowth that lies between the Wells road (which dates from the Turnpike Trust) and the much restored weavers' cottages of Darshill, it is still possible to find the remains of the leat, fed by a mill race still running as a perpetual waterfall, which powered the largest of the silk mills. The energy of that water is now spilled into the Sheppey, which in its turn once powered at least four cloth mills to the west in the village of Croscombe, before losing itself in the rhynes, as the drains of the Somerset levels are called. There is a local tradition, but no documentary proof, that the Shepton silk mill produced Queen Victoria's wedding dress. There is no doubt, however, that by the middle of her reign, the industry was already in decline, brought about by the riots caused by the introduction of machines. The military were called in to restore some sort of order, but the mill owners were content with the wealth they had amassed and on the whole preferred to close the mills rather than persist with their technological improvements. The Darshill silk mill was one of the few to continue working. It did not close down until 1913, and in the 1980s there were still a few old ladies alive in Croscombe who had worked there in their youth.

Croscombe was once a lively cloth centre. The remains of its industry are still visible in the traces of drying terraces on the hillsides on either side of the valley in which the village lies; and in the old mill chimney in the centre of the village, where the leat that once powered its undertakings rushes past the village school. The ruins of one of the largest cloth mills survive beside a house which was built in 1904 against the old drying shed, whose bricks are spaced with vents to provide a continual through draught. Popular belief has it that this was where the teazles (used to bring up the nap on the cloth) were dried. But that seems unlikely. The door is far too low for a stook of teazles to be carried through, and it seems more reasonable to imagine that the building provided further cloth drying space. On the hillside above this complex of modern domesticity and industrial archaeology, traces of the original highway can be seen running along the contour of the hill, for the road which goes through the valley as the A371 was only brought into existence with the Turnpike Trusts.

Mendip water power was also used in the production of gunpowder, and, by a similar process and for gentle contrast, snuff. These activities mostly took place in the Chew valley. Here the leats and ruins of the old mill workings can still be seen, together with the barns in which the nitre and sulphur were stored. Compounded with charcoal these substances produced gunpowder used for military purposes from the later Middle Ages to the Napoleonic wars, as well as for blasting rock and boring tunnels through the hillside. In the mid-nineteenth century these mills were put out of business by an Act of Parliament which authorized the Bristol Waterworks to build a pipeline carrying the waters of the Chew to Barrow reservoir on the outskirts of the city. Part of that pipe is still visible, a beautifully ornate aqueduct carrying the water aloft through the woods of East Harptree by the overgrown earthworks of Richmont Castle.

Its elaborate ironwork is a reminder that, as steam augmented water power, the Mendip mills began to work on another of the hills' resources. The iron in this region is something of a mystery. It is clearly visible in exposed surfaces of limestone, but no one seems to be quite sure what source was exploited in the nineteenth-century edge tool works. Writing in the early years of this century, Frank Knight reported that "some iron in the form of ochre" was being mined on Western Mendip; and John Cornwell of Bristol who has been responsible for organizing most of the industrial archaeology around Mells, believes from the evidence at Wookey Hole, Cheddar and

Charterhouse that at one time the iron workings on Mendip must have been as important as the lead mining.

Other iron pits are shown on the tithe maps for Stoke St Michael near to the sites of Fussells' main edge tool works. In 1500 Mells seems to have been known as Iron Burgh, but it was not until 1744 that the Fussells took over the derelict iron works run by James Naylor and started to make their fortunes. The family set up further businesses in Great Elm, Chantry, Railford and Nunney; and by 1857, James Fussell was rich enough to build the church and school at Chantry as well as a fine mansion.

His school was truly comprehensive. It combined an infant school, national school, industrial school and boarding school for girls, which was a fine source of good domestic service in the area. It has been immortalized in *Comin' Thro' the Rye*, a rather tedious romantic Victorian novel, written entirely in the present tense by the flamboyant Helen Mathers.

Fussell's mansion overlooks a lake, which served the dual purpose of pleasure and business. A carriage drive could be taken along its shores, and elegant picnics held in the fantastic Italianate grottoes, which today's children know as "the caves"; while its waters powered the production of scythes, hay knives, reaping hooks, bill hooks, axe-heads, spades, shovels and all manner of garden tools. "Nose to the grindstone" is a literal description of the fearsome conditions that the iron workers had to labour under, but the stone buildings in which they worked have been softened by time and decay into ruins that are as romantic as the lakeside follies. I think particularly of those that enhance a walk by Mells stream, through the garlic-filled woods of Wadbury valley.

The path along which the men from Mells set out to their work there, passes the overgrown quarry which provided the stone for the mill buildings, runs through the site of one mill (now some sort of unofficial centre for vehicle cannibalism) and then plunges straight into a Derbyshire dale. For this deep, narrow valley with its wooded rocks overhanging a fast flowing river is like no other place on Mendip.

A few hundred yards further on are the first signs of Fussell's main works, the walls of the old stores, carefully cleared by a group of dedicated amateur industrial archaeologists. The main works start at the place where the path leaves the stream, and runs behind the building which, once the offices of Fussell's works, now houses the equipment of those who give up their spare time to making this monument of the industrial revolution intelligible to the rest of us. Whether we have the technical ability to understand the processes that went on here or not, the place remains a mysterious romance, with the incessant rush of its millstream surmounted by the outlines of buildings, the different levels of which are joined by flights of slippery, narrow steps, softened by the indefatigable hart's tongue fern.

At its busiest time, 250 people worked on this site, and it is salutory to remember that the beauty of the place, if indeed it was so beautiful then, can have been of little account to those workers. The Reverend John Skinner, who came over from Camerton to visit Fussell's "Iron Valley" not long before the family gave it up, was saddened by what he saw, declaring that "we confine people in bonds more heavy to be borne than any of the most cruel of Indian planters ever imposed on their property".

Many city factory workers today, engaged in large-scale mass production, are descendants of the men who slaved in the nineteenth-century mills; but before everything became too large and uniform, Mendip had at least one individual contribution to make. The Mendip motor car is now as extinct as the Mendip sheep, the last specimen being ignominiously dug out of a hedge at Cookham near Marlow in 1967.

The car was evolved, and for several years produced, at Cutlers Green works at Chewton Mendip, which was established at the time of the Napoleonic Wars. In 1907 C. W. Harris, who then owned the works, designed a number of steam trucks that were shown at the Bath and West in the following year. In 1913 a Mendip char-a-banc was registered at Weston-super-Mare, and in the same year the first light car was produced, with the help of the local blacksmith. By the end of the First World War, the works were bringing out a model that could do 45 m.p.h. uphill, and a Miss Letty C., a physical education instructress, was so delighted with it that she took her car over to New Zealand with her for her marriage, despite some initial teething troubles. "Miss, first broke the differential, then each of the back axle shafts in turn and later one of the springs — so we changed the other three as well — and until we changed the gear box she was stuck on every steep hill," Arthur Thatcher, brother of the works manager at the time, recalled in his series of articles in *The Light Car* for 1972–3.

The Mendip car and Cutlers Green works are as though they had never been; and in time St Ivel's cheese factory at Evercreech, Showering's massive Babycham works at Shepton Mallet, and even the sinister military hutments of E. M. I. at Wells will all disappear. But they are unlikely to leave much fun for any latter-day industrial archaeologist. Today's utilitarian buildings are as uniform as the power that supplies them, and will vanish unmourned beneath the bulldozer when their time is done.

CHAPTER V

The Highways

NO TWO PLACES are alike on Mendip even if they serve the same purpose. I walk in the west along the ridge of Blackdown, keeping Rowberrow forest to my left and the hills of Wales on the horizon, until the path dips to climb on to the track that leads to the eastern entrance of Dolebury hill fort. Or I can make a harder climb of it, and storm its double ramparts by approaching it directly from the hill behind Rowberrow church. Either way I arrive at a rectangular enclosure, whose inner walls still stand up to twenty feet in some places. They enclose twenty acres, and the whole fort, like the prow of a ship on the edge of this spur of Mendip, commands a view that stretches west across the channel, and north to the lowlands around Congresbury.

Compare that with Tedbury camp in the east. It was built above the confluence of Mells Stream and Fordbury Water whose courses cut deep into the hills producing high steep banks that are a natural defence. So the camp's only earthwork, now gently wooded, lies to the south-west where the land rises gradually to Whatley. The flat defended area between the rivers is much larger than that of Dolebury, and during this century it has once again been used as a camping site. There is no wide view from wooded Tedbury. Its fascination comes from the waters which run far below it, and from a geological freak in the disused quarry at its eastern end, which has been worked down to the ancient sea bed, covered millions of years ago by the formation of dolomitic limestone, which accumulated in subsequent flooding.

Neither Dolebury nor Tedbury has been firmly dated, although it is generally supposed that they both belong to the Iron Age. Totally different as they are, they both serve the purpose of guarding important highways which could well have been in use from the paleolithic age. Dolebury, one of a chain of hill forts along the north of Mendip, guards a natural crossing of the hills from north to south, which the A38 still follows. Tedbury stands above the ridgeway running west from Frome.

No human activity can be carried out without some organized movement taking place, and in many ways that writing on the landscape is both the most fascinating of all, and the hardest to disentangle. The only certain thing is that men have been making highways over Mendip for thousands of years. Stone Age axe blades have been found here, which from their composition must have been brought into the area from Dartmoor, West Cornwall, the Lake District and Brittany; while flints, which could not have originated less than 25 miles away, have been found at Rowberrow, Cheddar Gorge and Priddy.

Like early people everywhere, those traders travelled along the drier ridgeways whenever it was possible to do so; descending the hills by paths which became hollow ways as successive generations of feet, hooves and wheels cut into the earth; and making summer tracks in fine weather along the lower contours. When a range of hills such as Mendip had to be crossed, they naturally took the easiest way between them.

In most cases the Roman engineers simply made good roads out of the routes which they found to be currently in use. So it was over such prehistoric trackways that the Romans who came to work the lead at Charterhouse built their arterial roads. At Bleadon, the Roman Road (still so-called) runs past an ostentatious modern villa guarded by two stone eagles. Supposedly built at the cost of some £300,000, its style suggests a mafia grandfather; it is not unfitting for it to be here, for its splendid views would make it the ideal site for any Roman official. That road continues along the ridge as a footpath incorporated into the West Mendip Way, a recently designated walking route. The Celtic Way, which joins the Roman Road, was once a hollow way running down the hillside. Bleadon is believed to form part of the route along which the lead from Charterhouse was taken to the port of Uphill. Nearer the mines, the road followed the prehistoric track along the ridge of Wavering Down, and as if in proof of that some Roman coins were discovered near the edge of a rabbit hole there, in the early years of this century. East of the A38, the route probably went over Shute Shelve to Callow Hill if it was wet, and by Winscombe Drove at the bottom of the hill in dry weather. There it joins the lane to Longbottom Farm, and the road that the nineteenth-century Shipham slaggers took to their work in the mines at Charterhouse and Priddy.

The lead may also have reached Uphill by being taken along the Broad Way which links the village of Shipham with the neighbouring hamlet of Star. From there it went along the present Shipham lane to

Sandford and Banwell. The remains of a Roman villa, in one of the most pleasant and sheltered valleys of Mendip, have been discovered on the south-facing slopes of Lyncombe Hill a little to the north of that route.

Although there is no conclusive evidence that the Romans shipped lead from Uphill, there is no doubt, from the pigs of lead that have been found to the south-east of the mines, that it was carried from Charterhouse to Old Sarum and so to the channel ports. The road running east from the mines used the prehistoric track along the ridge of Beacon Hill, the highest point on Mendip. There it crossed the Foss Way, on the stretch of that national road from the Humber, as it runs between Bath and Ilchester.

In the south-east of the area there were two further important junctions. At Cloford the lead route crossed the ridgeway road that runs south-west from Frome, and which is virtually covered by the A361; and near Witham Friary it met the Harroway, the prehistoric long-distance route from Kent to Cornwall.

From the time the Romans left until the start of enclosures and the formation of the Turnpike Trusts, the roads, such as they were, were a matter of local responsibility. For the most part they presented a real danger to travellers, and it was not unknown for people to be drowned on their overland journeys. There were only a few exceptions to that general state of affairs. On Mendip a few roads seem to have been kept in a reasonable condition by the Saxons, during the time that they needed to move the army in response to Danish invasions from the east and north.

Apart from that military use, the main traffic on the highways consisted of droves of sheep and cattle. Many ridgeway roads, I think especially of the one going to Frome over Beacon Hill, still have the wide verges which were allowed for grazing beasts. Here between hedge and road it was at one time allowable for anybody to build a house, provided that the building was completely fashioned between the sunrise and sunset of one day, with smoke coming out of the chimney at nightfall.

Other roads were never more than narrow green lanes along which strings of packhorses and donkeys carried immense loads of lead and coal, as well as the more manageable wool and corn. Some of their ways still survive as footpaths and farm roads. That is what has become of the main packhorse route from Cheddar to Bristol, which climbed steeply over the hills going north past Tyning's farm. In later days that route at least avoided the tolls of the turnpike road through Cross.

The long-distance packhorse ways were interspersed with shorter routes connecting one or two villages, or used for specific purposes. One footpath represents the coffin road along which the villagers of the hilltop village of Priddy used to bring their dead for burial at Westbury-sub-Mendip. Other lanes and paths, such as the Fullers Lane, which goes from Winscombe church to the Axbridge road, still carry the memory of the workers who trod them.

Some road names go back to the Saxons. Shipham, Cheddar, Churchill and Holcombe all have Lippiatts, literally "leap gates", an early form of cattle grid dividing their lowland and upland grazings. At Ebbor Gorge, above Easton the site is still known as Deer Leap, and two stone pillars in a field mark the place where the gate separated village and common land. That was the purpose of the Lippiatts, the agile deer could leap from one side to another, the cattle and sheep were confined.

Another reminder of the old routes and their traffic is found in the few bridges of Mendip, which often remain long after the roads they linked have all but disappeared. One of the most charming of these is Coleford's Packsaddle Bridge over Mells Stream, which now serves a little-used footpath to Leigh Upon Mendip. These little bridges had to carry heavy loads, with the full panniers or crooks carried by continual files of packhorses swinging above their low parapets. So they were sturdily built, and the fourteenth-century bridge at Pensford, with its two pointed arches, survived the torrential rain of July 10th 1968 which swept away the modern road bridge. The steep arch of The Bow, Bruton's packhorse bridge, has been less fortunate, for the force of the artificially narrowed river as it runs through the town has shattered it more than once of recent years. The four arches of the Tun-bridge at Chew Magna have made a better job of managing the fluctuating flow of the river. That bridge was built for heavy loads, and it still carries more traffic than its builders could ever have envisaged, but fortunately the main route through the town, which Collinson knew as the Portway from Wells to Bristol, makes use of another less venerable bridge.

Inns are often more long lasting than bridges, but not all The Nag's Heads that used to serve Mendip's packhorse men and their animals have survived. I think of one, which is now the central ruin of a sad row of derelict but sturdy cottages facing a little patch of green, on which a goat sometimes grazes, on Wells' Bath Road. The little group is rapidly falling into decay, awaiting its final blow from a greedy developer. That will happen as soon as the last tenant leaves. Her cottage stands next to the inn, where the Radstock men used to stop with their packhorses when they brought the coal into Mendip's city. The Globe, which is now my neighbour in Priest Row, was one of its rivals. It still has the drains where the mules and packhorses stood. They run beneath the rings on the walls to which the beasts were tied as they munched through their nosebags. Isaac Gregory, constable of Frome at the end of the Napoleonic wars, had cause to mention the Radstock carriers who frequented the Packhorse Inn in that town.

Outside the major towns other packhorse inns still flourish. The most notable of them are the three inns on the heights of Mendip, one at each of the three crossroads on the Old Bristol Road out of Wells. At the Castle of Comfort, the Miners' Arms (now an expensive restaurant), and the Hunters' Lodge — as you go from north to south — lead miners, shepherds and packhorse men drank together at all hours and in all tempers. Hunters' Lodge, run by Diana Dors' brother, Roger, is the favourite pub for the people from the cities who come to explore the surface and underworld of Mendip. You can get real ale here, and beautiful opaque green farmhouse cider which tastes almost as good as it looks. This is the inn the cavers use, and it takes some persistence to squeeze into it on a Friday evening.

The counterpart of these inns on the Old Bath Road out of Wells is the gaunt, uncompromising Slab House Inn. Its name comes from the slab which once stood beside it so that traders who did not want to visit Wells at times of plague could leave food on the stone. Like the inns to the west, Slab House is surrounded by tumuli, a sign that it stands by a trading route that has been in existence at least since the Bronze Age. Indeed it must have been a thoroughfare long before that, for this is an area where neolithic flint implements have been found, and they were brought on to Mendip from the Wessex chalk.

Barrows as much as bridges and inns point to the routes that people have taken over the hills for millennia. In their original state, before they were covered with earth and turf, the barrows were a form of waymarking for Bronze Age travellers. At a much later date, imported trees such as Scots pines, distinguishable even at dusk and in the clouds which so often cover these heights, were planted for the same purpose. On Shute Shelve and Callow Down they mark the drove route to the south coinciding with the miners' road or "slaggers' path" to Longbottom and the Charterhouse mines. But from pagan to Christian times the most reassuring message to a traveller came from stones and crosses.

Only one significant way-mark of that sort survives. I try to imagine the earthworks on Beacon Hill, on the largest of which the tall marker stone stands, clear of the surrounding beech trees. They make the place invisible from the road, along which the Romans took their lead to Old Sarum, and which crosses the Fosse Way at this point. The trees make an impenetrable screen even in winter, when they stand in a morass of mud among their own shed leaves, appearing to signal with gaunt, contorted arms. If they were not there the stone would be making its own signal south to Shepton Mallet and north along the Fosse Way (where travelling people now have a permanent site for their television-aerialled caravans) to Oakhill and Radstock. In the past the Beacon Hill stone could have been almost as compelling a landmark as the B.B.C. radio mast on Pen Hill, whose glowing red lights now guide the night driver back to Wells.

Other stones and crosses remain in name only: Longcross a couple of miles east of Beacon Hill and Susanna's Cross to the north of it by Stoke St Michael are at least marked on the map. Others have disappeared even more completely, and we only know of their existence from old records. Somewhere among the stones of farm buildings must be the twelfth-century Melewei Cross which marked the Saxon milkway above Cheddar. The same fate probably overtook Hopwells Cross and Boultings Cross on the wooded hill at the back of Compton Martin, Meer Oak Cross at the head of Longbottom, Smetcombe Cross near the neolithic henge of Gorsey Bigbury, and Nedge and Tor crosses which once marked the edge of the Mendip plateau above Wells. At least the fact that they were recorded makes it a little easier to work out how the main thoroughfares ran across the hills.

Many of these crosses, and indeed the old roads themselves, served as indicators of parish boundaries. The ridgeway path on the height of Wavering Down has marked the northern boundary of the parish of Compton Bishop for centuries, a long stone wall emphasizing the division. It is now a more serious and contentious boundary, for it is here that Somerset meets the new county of Avon, which it was mutilated to create. A little to the north-east Compton Martin is divided from West Harptree by Stratford Lane, the old Roman road which runs across the fields to the Blue Bowl Inn, and from there down to Chew Valley Lake. Once it served the Roman villa, whose excavated remains lie beneath Bristol's water supply.

None of these roads were shown on any map of Mendip until the end of the seventeenth century. They were routes known only to the people who travelled along them regularly. For the rest of the world, Mendip was a dreary wasteland to be avoided as far as possible. As late as the eighteenth century, when the turnpikes were already under way, a traveller as hardened as John Wesley supposed that Midsomer Norton was so called because it was impossible to visit it at any other time of year. The average speed for a horseman, familiar with the country, was never much more than five miles an hour at that time. Dr Claver Morris, who practised as a physician in Wells some 50 years before Wesley visited Somerset, reckoned that it took him some three or four hours to make the seventeen-mile journey to Frome.

Travelling began to get a little easier when the Turnpike network became established. The Bath Trust set up in 1707 was Mendip's first Turnpike road. It ran over Old Down, where the coaching inn now displays a copy (made by the wife of Robin Atthill) of a painting originally produced in 1769. It shows the kiln and brickyard close to the inn, both of which were marked on the 1817 Ordnance Survey map, but it cannot convey the difficulties which those apparently complacent early travellers had to undergo on their journeys. For within a couple of miles of Old Down the coach road branched into Bakers Hill. That incline is so steep that the passengers had to get out and walk, and even be prepared to help push.

The Bristol Trust was formed in 1727. Wells and Shepton Mallet were turnpiked in 1753, and for the first time a road ran through the valley of Croscombe. Bruton and Frome followed in 1756, Radstock in 1768 and West Harptree in 1793. Finally in 1827, the Wedmore Trust turnpiked the road through Cheddar to meet the Bristol to Bridgwater road, and in 1841 the Wells and Highbridge Trust took over the Wells to Cheddar road, which winds under Mendip's southern escarpment.

The Bristol Trust crossed Mendip by three roads that are still in use: the A28, the A37 going through Pensford and Farrington Gurney, and the steep lanes, known in Wells as the Old Bristol Road, which run past the Priddy mineries and over the border of Avon to Dundry. In the eighteenth and nineteenth centuries that road serviced the lead mines, as the Frome Trust in the east, which turnpiked the ridgeway road to Wells through Whatley and Little Elm, provided carriage for

Fussell's edge tool works at Nunney and Mells and for the collieries at Coleford.

The new road building required the construction of some new bridges. The most magnificent was Shepton Mallet's Waterloo Bridge, a span of 42 feet to the north of the town. It was built in 1826 to avoid the steep and dangerous road to Bath and Bristol; and John Farbrother reported that the festivities at its opening, the decorations, processions, fireworks and dinners rivalled the celebrations for the opening of the railway.

The coming of the stagecoaches produced a new generation of inns, some of which have now disappeared. In 1739 one was built to the north of Frome bridge (probably where the telephone exchange stands now) and used as the London coach office. It was called Champney's Arms after the owner of the site. Another vanished coaching inn was the First and Last at Croscombe, which closed in 1910. Many of the inns, like the one at Old Down and the George and Dragon at Pensford, still flourish while at least one toll house, Tucker's Grave at Faulkland, has become a pub, and still trades under that lugubrious name. At Cross, the New Inn with its beer garden and children's swings gives present-day tourists to the West Country the same sort of break that it once afforded to the passengers on the stagecoaches between North Devon and London. Nearly all the coaching inns served the purpose of stations. Each coach service prided itself on its time keeping, and the cost in the lives of horses was prodigious. In 1739, the Flying Waggon left Frome at 1 a.m. on a Monday and arrived at the King's Head Arms, High Holborn, by noon the following Wednesday, a reasonably leisurely journey necessitated by the awful state of many of the roads. One hundred years later, thanks to Macadam, the up mail from Exeter was calling at Wells at 4.55 p.m., reaching Old Down at 5.35 p.m. and racing through the night got to the G.P.O. in London by 6.51 the next morning, making the almost unbelievable average speed of ten miles an hour.

The turnpike roads were for long distance traders. Local people might be prepared to pay the lower tolls when their packhorse crooks were empty, but they were loath to pay double for a full load, and usually made the journey home by harder but cheaper routes. So while the various coaching companies competed for the carriage of passengers and goods on long journeys, and eventually set up horse-drawn omnibus services on shorter routes, the local village carriers plied their trade along the quieter side roads, leaving the toll roads to the larger carrying services such as the one that operated from Wells in the 1860s, departing from the Crown Inn promptly at 7 a.m. every Tuesday and Friday and taking goods along the road to Weston-super-Mare.

Mendip's system of water transport has vanished now, but not completely without trace. The Axe was once a navigable river, and in the Middle Ages overseas trade was carried out from the port of Rackley, which is now a farm by the side of the old river, whose main course has been diverted to the south-east. It lies below Crook Peak and a little to the west of Axbridge, which also had its wharves. There is evidence that a French boat came to that town in the fourteenth century; and in 1388 Thomas Tanner, a Wells merchant, used the Rackley wharves for exporting cloth and corn to Portugal, and receiving iron and salt in exchange.

Rackley was first mentioned in 1178, when it was set up as a port and borough under papal and royal charters, and described as Radeclive or Redcliff. For many years the lead from the hills was brought here, coming either direct over Callow Down, or being brought along the hollow way to the east of Cheddar at Redcliffe Street. Cheddar's own port was at Hythe on the road to Wedmore, and up to the early years of this century it was used as a convenient platform for washing sheep.

From the later Middle Ages, slate, salt and coal from South Wales were brought into Rackley and stored in the wharves there. The salt shed was still standing in 1915, when the Act of Parliament that covered the drainage of the Axe valley was passed. Then the flood gate at Bleadon was put up, and the wide stream of the navigable Axe flowing through wide swamps and marshes was transfigured to the tidy little canal that drains the fields today.

The seaboard of Mendip carried on trading for a few more decades. During the nineteenth century there was a coal wharf near the estuary of the Axe at Uphill, where up to 80 tons could be unloaded. That basin is now an anchorage for pleasure craft, which have just sufficient water at high tide to enable them to crawl through the mud to the channel. It is hard to imagine that in 1860 there was a grandiose plan for a harbour at Brean Down in which the Axe was to compete with the Mersey as Uphill became a rival port to Liverpool. The plan collapsed when the initial harbour walls were swept away by gales.

There are no navigable rivers in the east of Mendip, but just as the river transport in the west started to collapse, canal mania seized the whole country. They were seen as the obvious solution to the needs of the Somerset coal fields. Needless to say, John Billingsley was promptly in on the act. On the last day of 1792, he chaired a meeting at the Old Down Inn, called to consider the possibility of making a navigable canal to link the collieries with Bath. Talk was followed by action, and by the following autumn a plan was drawn up for a canal which would join the Western Canal, later renamed the Kennet and Avon, between Monkton Combe and Limpley Stoke. The actual surveying for the work was done by William Smith who came to Somerset in 1791, at the age of twenty-four, and was employed as surveyor to the High Littleton Coal Company. He was to become more widely known outside the county as the father of English geology.

The canal was authorized in 1794 and by 1807 it was connected to fourteen collieries, no simple achievement as there had to be 22 locks on the steepest part of its eleven-mile stretch. It was not only used for the carriage of coals. In April 1814, a group of Benedictine monks took a canal boat for the final stage of their journey from Shrewsbury to Downside; and once or twice it afforded the melancholy rector of Camerton a little pleasure. John Skinner could skate on it in winter, and in summer he organized a few picnic parties on freshly painted coal barges. They seem to have been rather grand affairs for he recorded in his diary for June 5th 1822 that on the return voyage from a picnic for which "there was an awning carried over the centre of the vessel and a table and chairs placed beneath", the Camerton band came on board at Dunkerton and "played marches and Scotch airs the whole way home".

A little further south the canal building scheme did not prosper so happily. On March 24th 1796 an Act of Parliament authorized an ambitious plan to link Bristol and Poole by way of Wincanton provided that an immediate start was made on a nine-mile branch from Frome to the collieries in the Nettlebridge valley. James Fussell's works at Mells were engaged in producing a sort of boat lift, a system of four balance locks which would get the water up Barrow Hill by Buckland Dinham. It was satisfactorily tested at a public display on the site on October 13th 1800. This was a feat of engineering skill comparable to that undertaken by William Smith and his colleagues of the Somersetshire Coal Canal in getting the barges up from Combe Hay to Dunkerton; but the proposed Dorset and Somerset canal never enjoyed its rival's prosperity. The money ran out. The course of the canal was cut, but it was never used.

The project has left its mark on the land, however, and it is still possible to take a tow path walk along some stretches of this dry and overgrown watercourse, by starting from the lane going north out of Great Elm and then taking the footpath that leads to the old ridgeway track towards Barrow Hill and its Saxon graveyard. The remains of the locks that carried the water up this hill lie close together in a wood a little to the south of the main path. No industrial archaeologist has as yet come to clear and tend them; and the surviving overgrown lock walls seem at first sight like some natural rock formation, even on the lower slope of the hill, where a small stream continues to trickle through the mud. Once on top of the hill, the course of the canal is clear for half a mile or so as a ditch runing a field away from the railway line. It disappears before the footpath reaches the lane to Buckland Dinham; but its signature can be witnessed once more as the Coleford aqueduct, which bridges a rift in the rocks to the south of the town. It was abandoned in 1803 and probably never carried water, but there's no way of even being sure about that. The only records of this canal that never happened were destroyed by the single bomb that fell in Wincanton in the last war.

The west of Mendip was not entirely immune to the canal fever although it had no coal fields to service. A survey was made for a route along the Cheddar valley but it came to nothing; more serious was the attempt to involve Mendip in the proposal to link Clevedon to the Tone at Taunton on a line more or less followed by the present motorway. The Parliamentary Act authorizing the work was passed in 1811 and a start was made on the Bridgwater to Taunton section. Several clauses in that Act caused consternation on Mendip. David Bromwich recently analysed them for the Banwell Society of Archaeology's journal *Search*. In Winscombe and Banwell the mill owners were anxious lest the proposed canal should divert the flow of water on which they depended. The vicar of Loxton was worried about the amenities of his parsonage, and backed by the Bishop of Bath and Wells he demanded that the canal company should buy his house for a sum that would enable him to build another, complete with a comparable garden and orchard. The Reverend David Stewart Moncrieff never got his new house. In 1841 the railway came to the western end of the Mendip hills, and the canal proposals were shelved.

Isambard Kingdom Brunel designed the Uphill railway cutting for the Great Western and the Bleadon road bridge that went over it. It was known as the Devil's Bridge and reputed to be the highest single-span brick-built bridge in the country. The railway was extended to Cheddar and Wells in 1870, tunnelling through the hill at Shute Shelve. This meant that Wells had three railway stations, each one managed by a different company, as the Cheddar Valley Line managed by the Somerset and Dorset railway company joined the Somerset Central and the East Somerset from Shepton Mallet. The Somerset Central came into Wells in 1862, climbing a 650-foot-high ridge before it could reach the city. Shepton Mallet nearly missed out on the railway prosperity, as one scheme after another had to be abandoned in the face of powerful opposition. However, on November 9th 1858 the North Somerset railway finally reached the town, and that was "a merry day for Shepton Mallet" as John Farbrother wrote two years later. The streets were "transformed into vistas of triumphal arches and festoons of evergreens" and one thousand shillings were distributed to the poor at Market Cross.

The railways soon found themselves in a position to service the collieries. The Somerset and Dorset bought up the Somersetshire Coal Canal and from 1907 to 1951 it was run as the Camerton and Limpley Stoke railway, with the line laid on the bed of the old canal. When the last colliery on that line closed on April 15th 1950, the service was reduced to one train a fortnight carrying farm equipment. By the autumn that run had been reduced to once a month, and the line finally went out of action in a blaze of glory as the setting for the film of *The Titfield Thunderbolt*.

Radstock remained a railway centre until March 1966, with the Pines Express from Manchester to Bournemouth going through the centre of the town each day. After that date, apart from a few stretches of freight line taking the stone from the quarries to the main line at Witham Friary, and a small portion of the old Somerset and Dorset servicing Harcroft Engineering works at Radstock, there have been no trains on Mendip. The railway age is remembered by a few derelict lines and cuttings; the private activities of the East Somerset railway manned by amateur enthusiasts from Cranmore; and the dramatic sixteen-arch viaduct at Pensford.

Today railway nostalgia is rife, but in the later years of the nineteenth century lovers of Mendip were crying with Theodore Compton, "Must we have our quiet meads and rural lanes disfigured, the field paths stopped by cuttings and embankments, the frisking lambs disturbed in their sports, the placid cows in their ruminations, and the feathered songsters of the grove scared away by the engine's frightful squeal?" Still, he was able to admit that when the "railway navvies have done their worst nature spreads her gentle mantle over man's rude works". He might have been pleased at the way gardens are encroaching along the old Cheddar Valley line out of Wells, and to know that in May 1982, Woodspring Council bought a length of line from Shute Shelve tunnel to the A38 in order to create a country walk, but he could never have become reconciled to the noise of the traffic on late-twentieth-century roads.

CHAPTER VI

The Marks of the Church

LANDSCAPE AND CHURCH are mingled here. Mendip's churches, as
well as its cathedral, are built out of stone from the hills, and with
their tall, square, castellated towers adorned with pinnacles at each
corner in the Somerset manner, they punctuate almost every view
across the countryside. And the land has affected Mendip's church-
men, from the twelfth-century Hugh of Witham, who returned to
his Somerset priory every autumn to refresh his spirits for his task as
Bishop of Lincoln, to the Victorian cleric, Augustus Toplady, who
was inspired to write the hymn "Rock of Ages" while sheltering
from a thunderstorm in a crevice in the rocks of Burrington Combe.

The bond between landscape and man's need to make holy places
was present here long before any churches were built. The three
stone circles which form the Bronze Age "church" of Stanton Drew
stand in farmland by the banks of the River Chew, along which rafts
probably carried them to their present site. It must have been a stupendous undertaking, putting even more strain on men and beasts
than the carriage of the stone from Doulting quarry to build the new
cathedral at Wells some three millennia later.

Unlike most other ceremonial sites of this date and scale, Stanton
Drew has no barrows or long barrows in its immediate neighbourhood. Their absence is remarkable. It could be accounted for by the fact
that on this fertile plain they were ploughed over; but it is more likely
that the stones served as a meeting place for the religious rituals of the
Mendip tribes, who preferred to have their chiefs' graves raised as
monuments on the hilltops. It has been estimated that there are ten
barrows to the square mile throughout the region. One of these
barrows, at Pool Farm near the Castle of Comfort inn, incorporated a
slab marked with a careful design of hollows and footprints. There is no
knowing what it was saying to the people who first saw it, but looking
at its replica in the little museum in Wells, it makes me feel that those
Bronze Age men had a special respect for the ground they walked on.

Apart from the slight ridges in the ground there is nothing to indicate to the casual walker that he is treading on ground that was sacred to Celts and Romans. But on Pagans Hill above Chew Stoke, the Romans of the third century worshipped in a magnificent octagonal temple containing figures of Hercules, Minerva and Mercury. Around it were the priests' houses and the guest rooms. Another Roman temple of the same date, but dedicated to Mars, has been excavated on Lamyatt Beacon to the south of Shepton Mallet; and a third from the fourth century has been discovered on Brean Down. There and at Lamyatt the archaeologists have found small east–west orientated buildings close to the original temples. They were probably the first Christian churches on Mendip. In both cases the nearby cemeteries, dating from the sixth to the eighth centuries AD, contained burials aligned in the traditional east–west Christian manner.

It was probably the Culdee missionaries, taught by the saints and scholars of Ireland, who first brought Christianity to Mendip. Crossing the channel from the beehive cells of the early Welsh monasteries they landed on the swampy shores of north Somerset. To the west of Brean Down, a rather nondescript little church serves the sprawling holiday camps and the few local people who live beside the sand dunes. It is dedicated to St Bridget, and every year on her feast day (February 1st) the people of Ireland send the vicar a traditional St Bridget rush cross to keep in his church over Candlemas. The Bridget they are remembering is the nun of Kildare who apparently never left Ireland. If any Bridget came to Brean, it could have been the one who is associated with St David's in Pembrokeshire.

Another Welsh saint who certainly came towards Mendip was St Cadoc. He used to leave his monastery to the south of Cardiff to seek periodic retreats, especially during Lent, on the island of Echni, now known by the more prosaic name of Flat Holm. Meanwhile his friend, the better known Gildas, was at Ronech (Steep Holm). There he built a cell and an oratory dedicated to the Holy Trinity. His twelfth-century biographer, Caradoc of Llancarfan, tells how the holy man would sleep on a steep cliff, a most dangerous thing to do above those racing currents. Gildas was forced to leave the island when pirates from the Orkneys raided the island and carried off his servants and their furniture.

The sixth-century St Congar also made a Mendip dedication to the Holy Trinity. He gave his name to Congresbury about 530, and possibly founded a monastery there. The tale that his father was

Emperor of Constantinople was probably an invention of his eleventh-century biographer. The tradition was that he came to Somerset in order to avoid the marriage that his parents had arranged for him with a heathen princess, or that he arrived less dramatically from the Levant on a trading excursion connected with Mendip lead. Another story gives him origins nearer home, declaring that he was the son of Geraint, King of Dumnovia (the tribes of Devon, Cornwall and western Somerset) who fought with Arthur against Saxon or Irish invaders at the mouth of the River Parret.

Wherever he came from, Congar spent most of his adult life on long missionary journeys throughout Europe, but however far afield he went he was beloved in Somerset, and when he died in Rome his companions brought his body back to Congresbury for burial. They are supposed to have laid it in a golden coffin and buried it beneath the yew he miraculously planted in the churchyard by beating the ground with his holy staff.

Somerset was not settled by the Saxons until after they had become Christian, and although the seaboard of Mendip suffered raids from the heathen Danes, there was no relapse into paganism during the Dark Ages.

A carved Saxon cross, displayed on the opposite wall, is the first thing to confront the visitor who opens the door of Rowberrow church, and others can be seen at Frome, Nunney and Shepton Mallet, while the church at Bleadon was mentioned as early as 956. More than two centuries before that the Saxon King Ina caused the first cathedral at Wells to be built, setting it up beside the springs that still bubble through the gravel basins in the shallow lake in the garden of the Bishop's palace. Ina was acting in the tradition of all the Celtic saints who sensibly made their Christian settlements beside the nearest available water supply.

In 909, Wells became the Bishop's see for the whole of Somerset, and for the next two hundred years the building of churches throughout the county went on apace. Several of them still carry their Norman features despite the Victorian improvers. The most completely Norman church is at Compton Martin, where St Wulfric (the anchorite of Haselbury Plucknett in the south-west of the county) was parish priest until 1125. The tiny church he served on Mendip is a minuscule Durham cathedral. One of its stocky pillars leans at an angle of 60 degrees, another has a spiral pattern around it, yet despite these oddities the little Norman arcade gives the impression of elegance and true proportion.

By the thirteenth century, church building was becoming more magnificent. Stone from Doulting was brought down the gentle slopes to Wells, and the present cathedral with its elaborate west front that can only be compared to Chartres, its incomparable chapter house and chancel steps and, literally above all, its four figure-of-eight reversed arches, which take the thrust of the building while serving as symbols of eternity, was completed under Jocelyn, first Bishop of Bath and Wells, in 1282. Fifty years earlier, on October 23rd, the day of St Romanus, the infant cathedral was dedicated to St Andrew. In the next century the 42 cells of Vicars Close were built for the choristers to the north of the chapter house. They stand now as substantial medieval houses topped by some of the first chimneys to be seen in England. The cathedral can boast Cardinal Thomas Wolsey and Archbishop William Laud among its bishops, but the most saintly men to hold the see fulfilled their office with far less worldly ambition.

Nicholas Bubwith (1407–1443) is still remembered in the name of the almshouses which he endowed for 24 poor men and women of Wells. In the early sixteenth century, Thomas Beckington, reputed to be the son of a weaver, was so generous in his arrangements for supplying the city with water that the fact was noted by Leland who came to Wells shortly after the Bishop's death. "There is a conduct in the market place," he wrote, "derived from the Bishope's conduct by the licens of Thomas Beckington, Bisshop sumtyme of Bath, for the which, the burgesses ons a yere solemply visite his tumbe, and pray for his sowle." The water that Beckington diverted still runs in the market square and down the streets of the city.

Best loved of all was Isaac Walton's brother-in-law, Thomas Ken (1684–1690), a man of strong principles, who was deprived of his bishopric because he found himself unable to swear allegiance to William of Orange, having already given his loyalty to James II. He was loyal to the Stuarts although he was often critical of their actions and policies. He enjoyed the patronage of Charles II, despite his uncompromising condemnation of that monarch's affair with Nell Gwynne, refusing to give her overnight lodging and declaring, according to his eighteenth-century biographer, that "a woman of ill repute ought not to be endured in the home of a clergyman". But in Wells, at any rate, he is remembered and still loved more for his personal generosity than for his public gesture.

His was no impersonal charity, for it involved him in regularly inviting twelve poor men and women to dine with him "always endeavouring, whilst he fed their bodies, to comfort their spirits by some cheerful discourse, generally mixed with some useful instruction. And when they had dined, the remainder was divided among them to be carried home to their families."

The portrait of this frail cleric, in the Bishop's Palace, shows a man whose compassion was tempered with austerity. The artist has caught an expression of determination rather than benevolence, although the eyes are kind. It fits in with a man who was concerned for the poor of Wells and who took their part against their exploiting employers; yet who was unsentimental enough to appreciate that some people could be made destitute by their own laziness and were primarily in need of rescue from bad habits and corrupting companions.

Having sworn allegiance to the established Stuart monarchy, he was naturally opposed to the uprising in support of the Duke of Monmouth, although he was well aware of the Papal threat presented by James II and was to be sent to the Tower for defying the King's wish to alter the constitution of the Anglican communion. His humanity was to override any political considerations, however. For after the fearful defeat of Sedgemoor he did all he could, both physically and spiritually, to ease the lot of the wretched prisoners herded into the great stone tythe barn by the moat. His action was all the more charitable because only a few days before these same men had torn down the figures from the niches in the west front as they camped on the Cathedral Green before the battle.

Ken was with Monmouth as he died, standing on the scaffold with him at the time of that cruelly bungled execution. He must surely have been responsible for the courageous way that the Duke met his death. When Judge Jeffreys came to Wells, ordering 97 people to be executed and 385 to be transported, having them driven like cattle across the Mendip hills to the Bristol docks, the good Bishop vainly tried to remonstrate with the tyrant and to insist that the offenders be tried by jury.

The first monasteries on Mendip were in the hands of Saxons. On Christmas Eve 885, Alfred granted a monastery at Banwell to Asser, his biographer, who also held a religious foundation at Congresbury. Even at that time the royal endowment of a monastery was closely tied up with extensive gifts of land, and from Domesday to the Dissolution, the history of the church on Mendip, as elsewhere, is linked to the story of land ownership. Much of Mendip land was in the hands of the Abbot of Glastonbury, the Bishop of Bath and Wells, and the

Carthusian Friars of Witham Friary and Hinton Charterhouse. Of these the Abbot of Glastonbury was the most powerful. He ruled an abbey that owned lands which reached north to Wrington, south to Batcombe and as far east as Mells, which was a regular stopping place for travellers on abbey business to Oxford and London. On other parts of Mendip place names such as Compton Bishop and Bishop's Chew (the old name for Chew Magna), as well as Charterhouse itself, still serve as a reminder of the church's wealth.

The Carthusians came to Witham Friary on January 6th 1182, making their home in one of the three monasteries which Henry II founded in penance for the murder of Thomas à Becket. In 1287 the friars who had also been granted land on the heights of Mendip acquired a licence to work the mines at Priddy and Rowberrow as well as at Charterhouse itself. The tradition is that their friary here was on the site of the Elizabethan manor farm which subsequently became a nineteenth-century mine owner's house, a private asylum, a sanatorium and finally, after a lapse of many years, a country club and private field studies centre.

Witham was the first Carthusian monastery to be set up in England, its church still serves the village of Witham Friary, but all traces of the friary itself have disappeared. A hundred years after its foundation, a second Charterhouse was set up at Hinton between Bath and Norton St Philip. It also owned land on the Mendip plateau, having a grange and pasture at Green Ore. The remains of the cells, which once housed twelve brothers and their prior, together with the grassed-over communal cloisters, the refectory and the chapter house, stand now on private land but they can be visited at certain hours. These buildings were excavated immediately after the last war, and services are now held here on midsummer's day.

Even small foundations could be tied up with land ownership, and in the west of Mendip, near Chew Stoke in the parish of St Cross, a cell of four nuns was founded near St Mary's Well, by Elizabeth de Sancta Cruce, whose family held lands in Moreton, Nemnet and Compton Martin. Nor was it only local monastic institutions that held Mendip land. St Augustine's Abbey in Bristol had pasturage for 50 sheep and 30 mares at Blagdon, and held a farmstead in that area.

The last monastery to be founded on Mendip was at Downside near Stratton-on-the-Foss, when the Benedictines of Douai bought the seventeenth-century Downside House of Mount Pleasant and started a school there. The building of the present abbey began in 1873.

The pilgrims on their holy journeys through Mendip were mostly bound for Glastonbury, as many of varying faiths and beliefs still are. Now they hitch hike over the hills from Bristol to Wells or Shepton Mallet, or drive their cars along the motorway towards Bridgwater and make the final stage of the pilgrimage across the levels. The memory of the medieval pilgrims who came this way from the Severn Estuary and the north is held in such lane names as the Pilgrims' Way in Chew Stoke. They came from the east, too, and the villages of Mells, Leigh-on-Mendip and Ashwick all had pilgrims' hostels.

There seems to have been at least one other goal of pilgrimage actually on Mendip itself. At Doulting above Shepton Mallet, the water springs out of the hill below the church. As well as starting a stream which once powered several mills, it provided a public well for the villagers, still approached by a lane whose ancient cobbles' recent macadamising was a sad desecration. Behind the well, whose waters are channelled through a wall, is the holy double spring.

On May 25th 709 Ina's brother, the gifted Aldhelm, died in the wooden church which stood on top of the hill on the site of the present building. This gifted and versatile man achieved a triple first. He was the first Englishman to write Latin verses, the first person to design an organ, and the first Bishop of Sherborne. He appears to have been beloved in his lifetime and so venerated after his death that people sought something of his sanctity in the waters of Doulting. Behind the crumbling walls of the vicarage garden which stand on each side of the public well, the springs pour out of the hillside to be caught in a stone lined basin running between carefully wrought shallow steps. Pieces of worked stone lie around, suggesting that at some time there was a building over the water channel.

The pilgrimages may have persisted after the Reformation but the power of Glastonbury as one of the greatest landowners in the country was gone for ever. Nor was it only the Abbey's wide acres that were disturbed. In the sixteenth century Somerset was not only the third most densely populated county in England, it was also the wealthiest after London. So there were plenty of people rich enough to squabble over the small but numerous parcels of land which came on to the market with the dissolution of the chantries in 1547. Most religious foundations maintained one or two chantry chapels, endowed by families who could pay for masses to be sung for their dead, and a certain amount of land went with each one of them. Wells Cathedral alone had nineteen such chantries.

The squabbles over land, which resulted from the dissolution of the chantries on a small scale, and from parliamentary rule on a large one, had no part in the third, more lasting expression of the break away from the established religion of the day: the rise of Nonconformity from its earliest stirrings in the seventeenth century. It was strengthened by those vicars, like Richard Fairclough of Mells, who felt unable to accept the Act of Uniformity at the time of the Restoration. He was forced to leave the village of which he had been a most conscientious parson for over forty years. As well as performing his Sabbath duties most meticulously he was in the custom of giving lectures to his flock on most weekdays, and started work at three o'clock every morning in order to prepare himself for these tasks.

The Congregationalists of Trudoxhill to the south-west of Frome still meet in the cottage in the centre of the village, which was converted to a place of public worship as soon as the 1689 Act of Toleration made that possible. They were not, however, the first group of Nonconformists to meet in the county. A few Quakers, no more than half a dozen or so, met in Frome from 1659, and ten years later a group of Baptists was formed in that town. By the eighteenth century the place was a mass of quarrelling and even violent sects. A preacher in Packhorse Fields was pelted with a variety of rubbish including mud and a dead cat. When Wesley came to Frome he found it a "dry, barren, uncomfortable place". He first preached there in 1752, and later confessed that he found it "exceedingly strange that any considerable good should be done at poor dead quarrelsome Frome".

Thirty years later, on September 7th 1785, he came to Mells and many of the hard-driven iron workers were converted. Their employer, Mr Thomas Fussell, was so impressed by "their changed mode of life" that he built a chapel for them and came himself to the service every Sunday morning and evening, making the journey from Wadbury House, about a mile from the village. This was no doubt all done out of genuine piety, but it must also have been a little gratifying to know how his actions would irritate the rival power in Mells. For the Horners, who were the lords of the manor at the time and not entirely well disposed to the Fussells and their works, made a firm rule of employing only Anglicans.

The nineteenth-century Anglican clergy like the disconsolate John Skinner, rector of Camerton, found the religious activities of the Methodists even more disturbing than the intractable irreligion of miners and farm labourers. Yet his diaries (1803–1834) show us how ill-fitted were the landed gentry, from whom the clergy were drawn, to communicate with the ill-paid workers who made up their congregations.

The result was that the established church tended to grow ever more negligent, leaving many parishes in the hands of aged, infirm or absentee vicars. Before 1857, the vicar of Winscombe lived in Wells. More understandably the rough areas of Rowberrow, Shipham and Cheddar, to which few constables dared venture, were left unattended. In such conditions Methodism flourished, a constant thorn in the flesh of those entrenched and harassed vicars who, according to their lights, were making an honest attempt to care for their flocks. Even the good works of the evangelical Anglican Hannah More did not escape their censure. Her work among the miners' families was feared as being Methodistical, and that meant that it was considered revolutionary and a threat to the very fabric of the British Constitution. Holding that view of Methodism, it must have been very trying for the established clergy that so many of the dissenters should be wealthy men like Thomas Ashman, the timber merchant, who built the Methodist chapel at Stoke St Michael.

The Catholics were in quite a different position. Those who chose to remain loyal to their faith met in small groups, people from Wells going to the chapel at Shortwood House between Lytton and Hinton Blewitt, a journey of some fifteen miles across rough hilly country. That chapel remained their only place of worship from 1785 to the building of the Catholic church at East Harptree in 1870. Mass was again said at Litton when the Irish navvies came to build the reservoir at Litton. There are accounts of them kneeling in the mud round the mill of Sherborne Farm.

The divergence in religious practice coincided with a growing concern for education. Many parish schools were established before the passing of the 1870 Act. In 1836, when a Tractarian Horner became prebendary of Mells, he started to loosen the feudal hold that his family had on the locality, and established a school in the village as well as a college for the training of missionaries and school teachers in the manor house.

Strangely the cathedral school at Wells, which now has a national reputation for the training of musicians, was not established until January 1881, although it was founded on a succession of choir schools attached to the cathedral. The other two religiously founded schools on Mendip, the Quaker School at Sidcot near Winscombe and the Catholic school of Downside, have a slightly longer history.

The site of Sidcot school was chosen in 1690, the year of George Fox's death when, on April 20th, Timothy Willis of Rowberrow handed over a cottage that he had bought, for use as a Quaker meeting house. The first school was started there in 1699 by William Jenkins of Hertford, who was invited to do so by the Bristol Friends; and the present foundation was soundly established on a co-educational basis on September 1st 1808, when nine girls were admitted to join the twenty boys.

The girls wore the traditional Quaker clothes, their wool dresses being of quiet colours, very full in the skirt and worn with a fine white handkerchief folded about the neck. Their bonnets were made of black or grey silk over a pasteboard frame. The boys wore nankeen breeches and had "bever" hats made of dog skin with the hair still left on. The boys and girls were kept quite separate. If they happened to meet by chance, the boy had to stand with his face to the wall, while the girl went quickly past him.

The children were nourished on beer made with two and a half bushels of malt to the hogshead. They had milk for breakfast, pudding and meat daily for dinner, and bread and cheese for supper. The regime at Sidcot was often as harsh as that of any other school of its time, being particularly Dickensian under the tyrannical rule of William and Mary Batt, who were its superintendents from 1821 to 1835. They introduced the barbaric "reflection boxes". Miscreant boys were sent to reflect on their misdeeds in these upright coffins, sometimes being confined in them for a couple of days at a time.

Good things happened at Sidcot none the less, even at the time of the Batts. The harshness of their regime must have been somewhat mitigated by the headmaster who ruled with them. Barton Dell started the school printing press and designed the Sidcot fives tower, so enabling the boys to join in one of Somerset's favourite games. In the second half of the nineteenth century, Theodore Compton, whose book on the Winscombe area of Mendip is still treasured, taught drawing and painting. Frank Knight, the other celebrant of Western Mendip, was among his successors, and he also wrote the present school song.

As I write, Sidcot's headmaster is Thomas Leindorfer, a Hungarian who came to this country in 1956. In 1983, when the school had 280 pupils, the boys still slightly outnumbered the girls, and only one fifth

of the children came from Quaker families. But the Quaker characteristic of individual responsibility is still an essential part of the school,
and Mr Leindorfer is certain that this independence will persist even if
the school eventually comes beneath the state umbrella. It is mainly a
boarding school, and pupils come to Sidcot from all over the world. It is
flexible enough to change with the needs of the society it serves, but
there are things that remain constant, and even a passing visitor would
have to agree with Nick Austin, head boy for 1982, who wrote in the
school magazine for that year: "Some aspects of Sidcot will never
change. Her position within the Mendip inevitably teaches an
appreciation of beautiful scenery." The quarry, which presents the
most immediate threat to that changeless beauty, is hidden by Callow
Hill. Fortunately under present local legislation it cannot encroach
further, but commercial lobbies are powerful, and the situation is
precarious.

Quaker meetings are still held regularly at Sidcot, but there it is the
school not the religious foundation that predominates. At Downside
the opposite holds good. The headmaster, Father Philip Jebb, a
grandson of Hilaire Belloc, claims that this is a monastery whose work
happens to be a school.

Father Philip has been at Downside for 40 years, and apart from his
student days at Cambridge he has spent little time away from Stratton-
on-the-Foss since he was a child. Yet the 580 boys here make up an
international community coming from as far afield as Africa and South
America. Their impact on the east of Mendip is as great as Sidcot's in the
west. Downside School has a great tradition of community service in
the area. It holds an annual fair to raise money for the pilgrimage to
Lourdes, which takes place every summer holiday; and there is a regular
programme of community service to the old and handicapped, and to
institutions like the Norah Fry subnormality hospital in Shepton
Mallet, the school for educationally handicapped children at Writhlington and the Cheshire Home at Timsbury. Both Downside and Sidcot
provide regular music and drama for people who must otherwise look
to Bath and Bristol for an experience of the arts.

A few miles across the hills from Downside Abbey is the newest,
smallest and strangest of Mendip's religious buildings. It stands in the
converted stable block at Ammerdown, home of the Catholic Lord
Hylton, and it is designed to serve all branches of the Christian faith
as well as being imbued with Jewish symbolism. That is partly a
contribution from the five nuns of Our Lady of Zion, who are based

at Ammerdown, and who belong to a hundred-year-old order founded to bring Christianity to the Jews. This is especially fitting, for the enterprise of which this chapel is the centre takes Mendip's St Hugh of Witham as its founder, who, while he was Bishop of Lincoln, was particularly involved in defending the Jews against their persecutors.

From Ammerdown, even more than from the Cathedral of Wells which serves the whole nation, some of the immediate needs of Mendip people, of whom at least two thousand were out of work in 1982, are met. In 1973, Lord Hylton, who inherited the estate in 1967, gave over part of his grounds for a residential study centre concentrating on the spiritual and secular needs of people living in rural communities. The centre is staffed by people of differing religious denominations and directed by a Methodist, Andrew Aldrich, an East Anglian and former Wiltshire Community Education Officer, who prepared himself for his work on Mendip by looking at similar rural communities in Yorkshire, Holland and Switzerland.

In 1978 he started work at Ammerdown, and the Hugh of Witham Foundation was formed with the practical aim of encouraging such secular village enterprises as the Oakhill brewery and the Ammerdown farrier, the main aim of such ventures being both to provide employment and to increase the vitality and sense of identity within the villages. This aim is also furthered by the encouragement of village celebrations based on the seasonal festivities of the Christian Faith, which naturally include a particularly joyous ceremony at Witham Friary on St Hugh's Day in November.

That saint is also remembered in the west of Mendip, where the tiny church that serves the scattered farms and cottages of Charterhouse carries his dedication. It was built in the early years of this century by a Cheddar curate who refused to take up the living of Blagdon unless it could also include churchless Charterhouse. Among the gifts that were made to that new church was the Rood Screen which came from the Hills family, whose own home of Hazel Manor at Compton Martin was burned down in March 1929.

There is no new church building on Mendip now, all the money and resources are needed to keep the inheritance of medieval churches in existence. The face of Wells Cathedral is almost permanently covered by the scaffolding of the restorers; while at the other end of the city money had to be urgently collected to save the tall tower of St Cuthbert's church, which has stood as a Mendip landmark for over six

hundred years. At the beginning of 1983 it started to crumble most
dangerously, and a fence has had to be put around it to stop visitors
approaching too closely. Perhaps all this shoring up is symbolic of the
churches' task in an age of general bewilderment, whose cause lies
outside Mendip but only as far as the British Aero-Space projects in
Bristol and the nuclear power station at Cannington.

PART TWO

PEOPLE AND PLACES

CHAPTER VII

From the Northern Levels

THE VILLAGE OF Wrington lies beside the drained wetland which fringes the north-western edge of Mendip as the Somerset levels do to the south. In its church porch its two most illustrious inhabitants are commemorated. One is the philosopher, John Locke, who was born in the village in 1632, and who recalled his homeland in his will, leaving £100 to the poor of Publow and Pensford where his clothier grandfather, Nicholas Locke, once owned a house. The other is the Bristol-born Hannah More, who made this village the base for her practical, evangelical philanthropy in the latter years of the eighteenth century. In both cases it was the families of miners and weavers who were the recipients of their charity.

A large monument stands over the grave of Hannah More and her four sisters who are buried together beneath one of the yews in Wrington churchyard. She died at Clifton at the age of eighty-two, but spent many years of her life a few miles from Wrington at Cowslip Green at the foot of the hills. It was that cottage which she took for her headquarters when she turned away from the literary society of London to start the work for which she is best remembered. As the author of *Percy*, a successful stage play, she was a close friend of the Garricks, Sir Joshua Reynolds, Horace Walpole, Dr Johnson and William Wilberforce. It was Wilberforce who convinced her that she should turn her talents to the service of the wretched poor of Mendip, most of whom were miners' wives and children.

Some of her best work was done in Shipham and Rowberrow where she found men and women "savage and deprived almost beyond [those of] Cheddar, brutal in their nature, ferocious in their manner". Undeterred by the fact that no constable dared venture into the village for fear of being killed and thrown down an old mineshaft, Hannah and her youngest sister, Martha, managed to open a school in the September of 1790. It took persuasion as well as will and courage to get it under way, for the wretched families could not understand the benevolence of these women, and were certain that they were "out to make their fortunes by selling the children as slaves".

The Mores had the good sense to realize that they were dealing with deprived rather than depraved people, and that the "deep and serious attention" which met John Wesley in Shipham when he preached there in 1782 could still be evoked. Hannah was not without the support of many of the villagers. She was able to give the charge of the school to Patience Seward, a dairymaid, who had formerly run a Sunday school for thirty children. Under Hannah's guidance, her half-sister Flower Waite worked with the girls, and William Wokey of Shipham and John Morgan of Rowberrow taught the boys.

The school did so well that in the summer of 1791 the children joined with those from the Sunday schools in more respectable parishes for a massive feast on Callow Hill, during which they were regaled with cider and beef and plum pudding. The outing was so unusual that the watchers are said to have outnumbered the children.

Two years later Hannah was congratulating herself that although her work was done in "a land of labour and vexation" there was hope, and "we have the certainty of much improvement in the knowledge of the scriptures, and great acquirement in reading". Her aims in education were certainly not designed to upset the balance of society but rather "to form the lower classes to habits of industry and virtue". In teaching the poor she wanted to "qualify them for constables, overseers, churchwardens, jurymen and especially tend to impress them with the awful nature of an oath". She was a firm opponent of the French Revolution, and it was claimed that her pamphlet *Village Politics*, written under the pen name of Will Crisp, helped to prevent a similar revolution in England. Not content with quietening the miners of Shipham and Rowberrow, she wrote a ballad called *The Riot* which she had set to music and prepared as a pamphlet for the colliers around Camerton and Radstock. It pointed out the folly of their intention of going on strike and attacking the local landowners, and it was undoubtedly instrumental in dissuading them from that action.

From the peace of Cowslip Green, and later on from Barley Wood in Wrington, Hannah rode or drove along flat winding lanes to the Mendip foothills, and up the steep, wooded slopes to the mining villages of Rowberrow and Shipham, places which had been settled long before the Romans came to exploit the mines. Bronze Age axeheads and delicate leaf-shaped arrows have been found on Callow Hill, and a little to the east, by Longbottom Farm, on the edge of the pine forest that now covers the medieval warren of Rowberrow, there is an Iron Age camp, which may well have protected the lead routes of Celtic miners.

On the other side of the village is the site of a Roman settlement of the first century AD. The villa was rebuilt in 300 and demolished some 50 years later. It must have been a pleasant place to live, for it stood in a beautiful and sheltered spot on the southern slope of Sandford Hill. It is now reached by a narrow, muddy, dead straight green lane, which leaves the main Bristol to Bridgwater road to the west of the Star Inn, which takes its name from Shipham's subsidiary hamlet. Before climbing up to the site of the villa, the lane crosses the valley watered by Pyle Well, once one of Shipham's main water sources, and now flooded into a marshy pond surrounded by yellow flags.

In the fields to the north of that pond is one of Mendip's rare standing stones, a massive chunk of dolomitic conglomerate, 5' 6" high and 6' 2" broad. To the layman, this massive, almost triangular slab, with a hole at its base, presumably caused by weathering, resembles a capstone. But there does not appear to be any grave or cist beside it. Over the centuries it has almost come alive, and now seems part of the field hedge it appears to grow out of, and to share in the life of the elder, hazel and hawthorn bushes that surround it. It belongs far more to nature than to the earthwork that runs across the field, and whose original builders could possibly have told us how the stone came to be there. As it is it remains a mystery. No one knows if it ever had any religious significance, or whether it is simply a very ancient boundary mark. In common with many such stones throughout the country, it is supposed to walk about in search of water, and from "wimble", meaning to "move lightly", it has been given the name of the Wimblestone. Tales of its wanderings are still told, albeit with some cynicism. One Shipham joke runs that it goes round the field every night when it hears Sidcot clock strike twelve — but, of course, stones cannot hear.

A little coal was found in Shipham in 1813 near the Longbottom hill fort; and it is still possible to trace the site of this long-abandoned mine, with its curving banks covered in purple lousewort. But it was mostly lead that concerned the Shipham miners, and for centuries nearly every man in the village earned his living down the pits. In the nineteenth century, those who were unable to find work nearer home took the "Slaggers' path" to Charterhouse, going along the Lippiatt and over Cock Hill to Longbottom and then east past Tyning's Farm to spend their days as diggers and furnace men for the Mendip Mining Company. When that closed down they went further across the hill to St Cuthbert's mine at Priddy. To get there they had to run the gauntlet of the Charterhouse women, who were anxious that their men should be the first to get to the working mine.

They must have been tough, determined ladies, for Shipham miners were relentless fighters, either among themselves or banded together in defence of their country. When Macaulay wrote of the Spanish Armada, he told how "the rugged miners poured to war from Mendip's sunless caves", and many Shipham names are to be found in the lists of Somerset men who went to London to enlist in 1586. A hundred years later their grandsons stood by the Duke of Monmouth in his ill-fated bid for the English throne, and at least one of them, Jacob Trypp, was tried and condemned by Judge Jeffreys at an emergency court in Axbridge. Three more generations went by, and the Shipham men were prepared to fight again, marching to Bristol to meet the threat of the French troops who landed in Fishguard in 1797.

Perhaps they felt that anything was better than the Shipham mines which dominated the village, and which have now vanished almost without trace. The gruffy ground which marks the scene of the greatest lead mining activity stands in neglected ground beyond the new housing estate, and cavers are the only visitors to the shaft of the Singing River Mine, whose entrance, to the south-east of the church, is carefully protected from casual explorers.

Although Shipham is largely a village for Bristol commuters and retired people, at least one active farmer lives in one of the comfortable new houses by the gruffy ground on Glover Field. George Thiery, whose Huguenot family originally sought refuge on Mendip after the siege of Nantes, is the grandson of one of the last men to work in the Shipham mines. Indeed, mining and farming were often linked operations, despite the bitterness that could flare up between individuals.

The residue of that bitterness centres on the danger that the defunct mines can present to stock. Although all the shafts were supposed to be filled in or walled round after the mines had been closed down, stories abound of animals falling into the pits. Mr Thiery had one in-calf heifer missing for nine days, and she was only discovered when a party of bird-nesting children stumbled by the place where she lay.

The Miners' Arms (not to be confused with the one near Priddy) is all that remains in Shipham now to show the passing traveller the nature of the village he is going through; but in the 1920s it could still justify its name. The manager's house at Charterhouse where the Shipham men worked was still standing on Ubley Rake, and the tall nineteenth-century chimney, known to local children as Julius Caesar because they knew that lead was something to do with the Romans, had not yet been demolished.

Cadmium as well as lead was mined in Shipham. The industry began in the late fifteenth century when the land was found to contain zinc, called calamine from the Latin *calimina*, a reed, because of the way the metal stuck in long reed–like strips to the furnace walls. By the late eighteenth century it was being used for the conversion of copper into brass, and to that end it was sent to Bristol for processing; only the washing of it was done in Shipham. That procedure is remembered in the name of Barnpool for the triangular piece of grass by the council houses. There was a pond here once and the calamine barn stood beside it.

By 1791 the calamine industry was at its height. Collinson found "upwards of one hundred of these mines now working, many of which are in the streets in the yards and some in the very houses". It probably would not have surprised him too much to learn that nearly two hundred years after he made that report, an elderly Shipham lady discovered a house mine shaft in front of her kitchen sink.

When Billingsley came to Shipham, a few years after Collinson, he noted that the calamine mines were seldom worked deeper than 30 fathoms. He reckoned that between four and five hundred miners were employed in the business and that the average price of the ore was £5 a ton. That meant that the miners could earn up to a guinea day, making them far and away the wealthiest men on the hills. The decline of the calamine trade came at the end of the Napoleonic wars, and Shipham slid from riches to poverty as nearly all the men in the village were thrown out of work. Their situation was slightly and temporarily relieved by Hannah More, who showed that she understood that practical economics had to be combined with charity. She bought up the ore that the Bristol processors were refusing and stored it away to await better days. Alas they never came.

It was not until the late 1970s that Shipham's name was linked with cadmium again, when a nationwide survey reported that there were unacceptable amounts of trace elements and cadmium in Shipham soil. The scientists moved in, Hoover dust was analysed and the villagers were told not to eat any green vegetables. Medical tests were done on their blood and kidneys. Monitoring of one sort or another went on for several years in what the media inevitably referred to as "a doomed village". But the inhabitants do not feel doomed. They claim that the local doctors find no evidence of any poisoning, and that the undertakers' records show that the average age of death in Shipham is some two years beyond that reached by Somerset people as a whole.

In defiance of the scare, Shipham gardeners have now instituted a "cadmium cup" for the winner of the vegetable competition in the local flower show; and although they admit to finding "the mineral" (lumps of yellow lead ochre) in their gardens from time to time they deny that it can be absorbed by the plants. Together with most people on Mendip they are now more distressed by the quarries than the mines. Two of these, one temporarily disused (a disabled man being kept on the payroll to prevent its final closure), scar Shipham gorge as you climb up to the village from the vale of Cheddar. The one that is still in operation, owned by English China Clay, has been eating away at the hillside since the 1920s, and lime was burnt on the site until 1969. This quarry is rapidly destroying Callow Hill in order to produce dry aggregate for road making.

All this industry, from the mines to the quarries, cannot obscure the fact that Shipham (as its name suggests) was once primarily an agricultural area. It still is, although now the cattle rival the sheep on the hills. In the Middle Ages when sheep predominated, Shipham sheep fair was quite as important as Priddy's is now. The church was almost as interested in its grazing grounds as in its mining rights. St Augustine's Abbey in Bristol owned a small sheep farm in Rowberrow, which was leased in 1407 to Walter Bevice of Wrington and Alice his wife. They had to supply the straw for thatching the sheep house, which remained in the Abbey's possession, and make half the hay crop from their farm available to the Abbot's sheep. In Wrington, the manorial accounts of that time relate to shepherding and the sale of wool, the sheep being grazed on the Shipham hills. Shepherding was no summer idyll; at the end of the fifteenth century a shepherd received 26s 8d a year, and part of his work was to drive the sheep over Mendip from Wrington to Glastonbury. He was paid an additional 3s 4d for his stay on the high ground, a fair measure of the discomfort he could expect to encounter there.

In those days sheep meant cloth, and Wrington's other contribution to that trade was the cultivation of teazles. It was never an easy crop to handle, the plants take two years to mature and can be completely ruined by one wet season; and the ground between the young plants has to be kept scrupulously clean. This was done with a special narrow spade in a process known as "speddling". The harvest took place in August when the heads were cut from the stems and graded as Kings, Middlings and Scrubs. The latter were of little value, but in Billingsley's time a pack of nine thousand Kings and twenty thousand Middlings sold for 40 shillings.

Some of these teazles might have been sold at Wrington's annual fair on September 9th, inaugurated by Adam de Sodbury, an early-fourteenth-century Abbot of Glastonbury. He also procured a Tuesday market for the village, which still went on after the fair was discontinued in the eighteenth century, although Collinson found it "very trifling".

Shipham's sheep fair was held on the last Wednesday in April, but long after it had been supplanted by the one at Priddy the even more important November Fair went on. It was held on the Feast of St Leonard to whom the village church is dedicated, and until 1927 it was the most notable local event of the year. There was a hand-turned roundabout in the square and stalls for fairings around the Miners' Arms. But the real business of the day went on at Fair Hill around Little Manor, an Elizabethan farmhouse, now an old people's home. George Thiery's father owned the place from 1907, having moved there from the farm of Penscot in the very centre of the village. That is a hotel now, and much used for special occasions. In the old days the November feasting went on at Fair Hill, when the business of the day was over and the villagers marched up the hill from the square to enjoy the ox roast. After the merry-making and the trading came the settling up. By tradition the owner of Fair Hill was "stake holder" for the fair. That is he had to supply the hurdles for the event, which he could then sell off for a pound a dozen when all the business was over. Mr George Thiery still remembers the first auctioneer to come to Shipham. He was a Mr Shiner, who had to endure a few years of uneasy competition before he was eventually ousted by the thrusting Mr Percy Palmer, whose firm of Palmer and Griffiths still trades as a local estate agent.

In the early years of this century, the roads around Shipham, which now carry the stone lorries and the cars of commuters and tourists, were busy with farm traffic all the year round, reaching its crescendo at fair time. Lime burnt from Callow rocks was sent all over the country and even shipped to America. The kiln fires were kept going night and day, only being allowed to die out at Christmas. Carting the lime about could be a hazardous undertaking. At least one wooden cart load was caught in a heavy rainstorm among the crags of Burrington Combe, with the result that the lime caught fire. In that case, the carter was fortunately quick enough to empty out his load and save his cart and horses.

Other carters went on overnight journeys from Shipham to Radstock to collect coal for the farms and cottagers. Even in the small hours, the Castle of Comfort on the Mendip heights beyond Priddy could be relied on to supply these travellers with a supply of warmed beer in a metal box, to sustain them as they made their way over the hills. Although it was made in daylight, the return journey was harder. For with their carts heavy with coal, the carters had to come back along the longer valley road by the Harptrees and Compton Martin, managing to unload a little at those villages before making the final steep climb up to Shipham.

Conversely the potatoes and vegetables that were taken from the four-acre allotments on Shipham Hill went along the lower road to the east, passing through Long Ashton in the early hours of the morning to catch the Bristol market and coming back empty up the steep hill past Dolebury.

Carts of lime, coal or vegetables sometimes found their way blocked by Bristol Billy, the drover who used to walk cattle through Shipham during the springs and autumns of the 1920s. They were Irish cattle he was driving, brought into Avonmouth and put out to graze for the summer in the fields around Wedmore. Cattle droving was a skilled and occasionally dangerous occupation. One of Billy's predecessors died in the Miners' Arms after being gored by a bull that ran mad in Shipham square.

Like all Mendip villages, Shipham and its neighbours had no certain water supply until the pipes were laid in 1915. Although the village was not short of good wells, many people had to make considerable journeys to collect their water. They fetched it from Grace Locke's Well on the top of Shipham Hill, which never stopped flowing even in the fierce drought of 1911; or they went west into the valley beyond Star to get water from Pyle Well near the Wimblestone. Special yokes were made for the children, who had to collect water from these wells before they set off for school. In Rowberrow, beneath Dolebury Hill, an artesian well maker from Easton, near Wells, bored for water. He was successful, and Rowberrow Manor is still allowed a free water supply in return for the facilities it allows to Bristol Waterworks, who use that source to pump water up to Mendip's highest land on Blackdown.

Between the tiny hamlet of Rowberrow, in whose churchyard at least one young man "crushed to death in a mine" lies buried, and the farms of Blackdown the land ownership has often been disputed bitterly. It is covered by the Forestry Commission's twenty-year crop of wood pulp now, but in the Middle Ages it was a rabbit warren, providing valuable food for its owners. The warren interfered with the grazing rights of the commoners, who were still complaining about this injustice at the end of the seventeenth century. They were particularly angry with a certain Jonathan Prickman, who "having neither Mannour nor Lordship on Mendip" had set up three warrens on the hills including one at Rowberrow. No doubt many of his rabbits were poached by the lead miners who would find them fair game on their way back from work. In 1795 there were still warrens at Charterhouse and Ubley, and by then, at a time of great rural poverty, the rabbits were no doubt at the mercy of starved farm labourers who felt it worth risking a heavy punishment if they could add something to the family pot.

At least the Rowberrow farmers had the right to cut the bracken, which still grows in abundance on the peat which has accumulated on the old red sandstone of Blackdown, and compress it for animal bedding, using a dray or sledge to haul it down the steep slopes of the ridge. Meanwhile their wives and children could gather whinberries, a laborious, slow and back-breaking job, which some people still undertake on a small scale. There's nothing to beat a good whinberry pie, although it does take a long afternoon's picking to make the baking worthwhile. But not so many years ago Blackdown whin-berries, picked for Robertson's jam factory in Bristol, were a modest addition to a family budget. That represented a month's rather than an afternoon's picking.

In the nineteenth century, on Mendip as elsewhere, women and young children expected to have to take on such uncomfortable hard work in order to keep the family going. In 1867 a parliamentary commission was set up to enquire into their employment in agriculture. North-east of Shipham, down in the Chew valley, the Reverend E. A. Ommaney, vicar of Chew Magna, reported to the commissioners: "Women work a good deal in the parish which is a large one [at that time it had a population of 1855] but they are of little good. The people generally are a lazy, idle set, and like dawdling about the parish."

On the southern side of the valley, the Reverend C. M. Nutt, vicar of East Harptree, was either a more charitable man, or more fortunate in his parishioners. He claimed that his village "has been called in the neighbourhood young Oxford. There is a fair National School and a large British School". Although the latter was "a great stronghold of dissent", he still regretted that he found it "difficult to interfere with the children going early to work. The parents require their wages".

He would surely have appreciated Guido Morris, who settled his Latin Press down on the levels at Langford, near Hannah More's Wrington, during the 1930s. He lived in Hick's Hay, a small white-washed cottage to whose door he had affixed the following broadside: "Guido Morris lives here with an army: the twenty-six soldiers of lead who can conquer the world and rout man's enemy." The villagers used to know him as Grub, because he used to tell them he was grubbing for a living.

Had he settled at Langford ten or twenty years later, his un-English Christian name at least would have caused no surprise. Many Italians and Germans came to work on the Mendip farms during the last war, the Youngs had groups of them living in their Shipham cottage while they were farming Lower Farm. But it was mostly the Italians who stayed on, married Mendip girls or brought their own families over from Italy, so that in this area it is very common to see Italian names on trade vans.

CHAPTER VIII

The Forest of Mendip: Axbridge, Cheddar and Wells

THE OLDEST TRACES of human life in Britain were found in 1969, when a large unroofed cave was discovered in the quarry a mile above the village of Westbury-sub-Mendip, which lies beneath the southern cliffs of the hills. That cave was occupied some 300,000 years ago, during the Early Ice Age. Bones of bears, lions, Etruscan rhinoceros, bison and many small mammals were found in it, but the most exciting discovery were the rotted remains of worked flints, proving that men had coexisted with these beasts, and that Mendip's human history goes back to geological time.

Those very early hunters were the forerunners of generations of privileged men who had an exclusive right to hunt wild animals in the Royal Forest of Mendip from the time of the Saxon kings to the end of the Middle Ages. It was in Cheddar that the Saxon kings of Wessex had their palace, and royal hunting lodges were built in the area around it from the time of Alfred. According to the fourteenth-century Axbridge chronicle, King Edmund "used sometimes for the sake of hunting to spend the summer in the Forest of Minndep, in which there were then a good many deer and different sorts of other wild animals".

The chronicle goes on to tell how an alarming adventure befell the tenth-century Saxon king, Edgar, soon after he had bitterly and, as he thought, irretrievably quarrelled with Dunstan, Abbot of Glastonbury, banishing that holy man from his court forever. During a hunt, the king followed a stag to the very edge of Cheddar cliff, and was only saved from plunging over the rocks himself by his horse miraculously stopping at the very spot over which the stag had fallen to his death. The king, feeling that his own life had been spared by an act of God, told the story of his escape to the nobles assembled at his Axbridge hunting lodge, and commanded that Dunstan be brought back into favour.

Edgar's adventure was no doubt frequently repeated throughout the centuries, not always with such a happy outcome, for the Mendip plateau where most of the hunts took place runs smoothly to the towering pinnacles above Cheddar Gorge. In 1895 the entire pack of Wells' harriers were lost over the cliff.

After the Norman conquest the bounds of the Royal Forest land on Mendip fluctuated with the greed of the kings. At the start of Henry II's reign in the middle of the twelfth century, the bounds were extended northwards as far as Winscombe, and John, always hungry for more hunting land, made further excursions into the estates of lords and commoners. Under the ten-year-old shadow of Magna Carta, Henry II promised that any woods which the monarchs had encroached upon since Stephen's reign should be restored to their rightful owners. His promise was not completely fulfilled. A document of 1290 in Wells Cathedral library gives details of the feudal obligations of one Thomas Well, who held one virgate (40 acres of land) in Winscombe, on condition that he did not marry his daughters without licence.

Eight years later, when Edward I sent a commission to examine the bounds of the Somerset forests, the manor of Winscombe was freed. The true limits of the forest land were then defined on May 10th of that year, and again two years later when a perambulation of the bounds was carried out by two knights of the shire representing Sabina Peche, a remarkable woman for her times in that she insisted on claiming her hereditary rights as chief forester of Somerset. That meant that she had power over both Exmoor and Mendip. The party making the perambulation was quite impressive, for Sabina's chief representatives were joined by two verderers, a jury of five knights and seven gentlemen of the forest.

The church as well as the people were involved in forestry disputes with the king. These disputes became particularly bitter when Ralph of Shrewsbury became Bishop of Bath and Wells. In 1322, Matthew Peche (Sabina's grandson), Robert Atte Box, John Knyghte, Clement the Forestarius and John Champyon the Forestarius quarrelled with the Bishop because his men had been fetching wood for fuel from the Bishop's boscus at Biddlecombe near Wells, which was overlooked by the Royal Forest and considered to come under its jurisdiction. In December the Bishop retaliated by attempting to excommunicate three of the foresters if they would not perform public penance in Wells Cathedral and in the churches of Cheddar and Axbridge respectively. This penance consisted of standing barefoot by the font in a penitential attitude, clad only in a shirt and holding a lighted taper in one hand.

This seems to have proved too much for John le Knyghte, for Robert, the vicar of Cheddar complained that he did not hold his candle, nor did he stand in a place where "the congregation might be the better able to see him". However, Edward III took up Knyghte's cause and was properly furious at the way his foresters were treated. In the following January he wrote to the Bishop from York to say that his three men were completely in the right and that Ralph's men had to be prevented from cutting down trees "in the wood of Chedre, within our forest of Menydeep". Nevertheless, it was during Ralph's time that the deforestation of Cheddar Manor gradually began.

Until that time the Cheddar oaks were in the king's gift, and had been so long before Henry III gave fifteen of them to a master carpenter for his work in repairing the royal mills at Huntspill. And whatever the rights and wrongs of the forestry disputes, it was the trees and so eventually the land that suffered. By definition a "forest" does not necessarily mean a wooded area, but land outside normal jurisdiction. Nevertheless the Forest of Mendip was once wooded, and the destruction of the trees, first for building and then to fuel the smelting furnaces for the lead, began the process of degrading the hills that the quarries are now carrying on.

Mendip began to be deforested in the sixteenth century, but now some of the land is once again in the hands of the Crown. For part of it has been taken over as a rifle range. Although some of that land is still farmed, the public footpaths which represented the old "chimmin-age", or rights of way through the forest, are lost; and the "Danger Area" marked on the Ordnance Survey map extends past Stowbar-row, one of the boundary marks of the Forest of Mendip mentioned in the medieval perambulation of the forest. Even more acres are held by the Forestry Commission, which set out by planting conifers instead of the broad-leaf trees which are native to the hills.

Some of the old Forest of Mendip remains, available for people to enjoy, bare of trees as it is. It was the Saxons who by over-cultivation eroded the land around the village of Compton Bishop, which lies in the folds of the hills beneath Crook Peak and Wavering Down. The lower lands of that village are now being intensively farmed, but there are few better places for a summer walk than the treeless uplands.

Crook Peak gets its name from the rocky outcrop at its summit, which gives it the false appearance of being the highest point on Mendip, and which is said to resemble a "Crook" or packhorse saddle. It was once a notable Beacon hill, forming part of the chain of signals which ran westward to Exmoor's Dunkery. A note in the Banwell

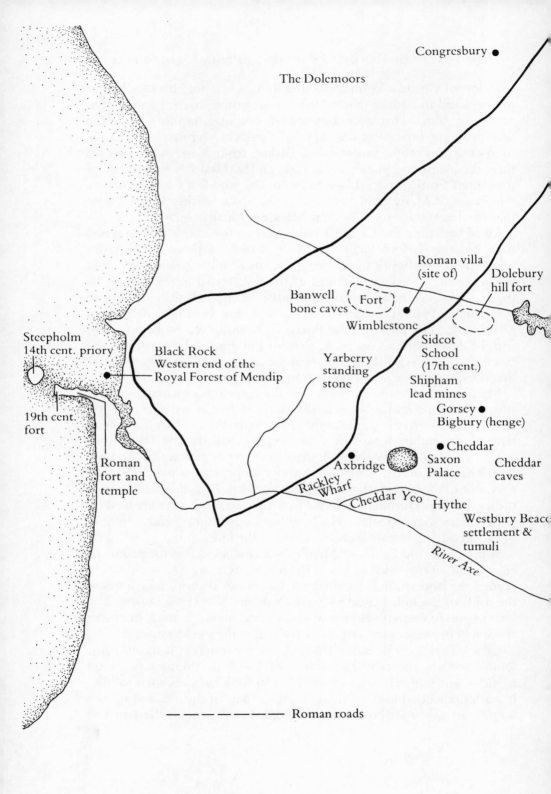

Congresbury

The Dolemoors

Roman villa
(site of)

Dolebury
hill fort

Banwell
bone caves   Fort

Wimblestone

Sidcot
School
(17th cent.)

Shipham
lead mines

Steepholm
14th cent. priory

Black Rock
Western end of the
Royal Forest of Mendip

Yarberry
standing
stone

Gorsey ●
Bigbury (henge)

19th cent.
fort

● Cheddar

Axbridge   Saxon
Palace

Cheddar
caves

Roman fort and
temple

Rackley
Wharf

Cheddar Yeo   Hythe

Westbury Beaco
settlement &
tumuli

River Axe

— — — — — — — Roman roads

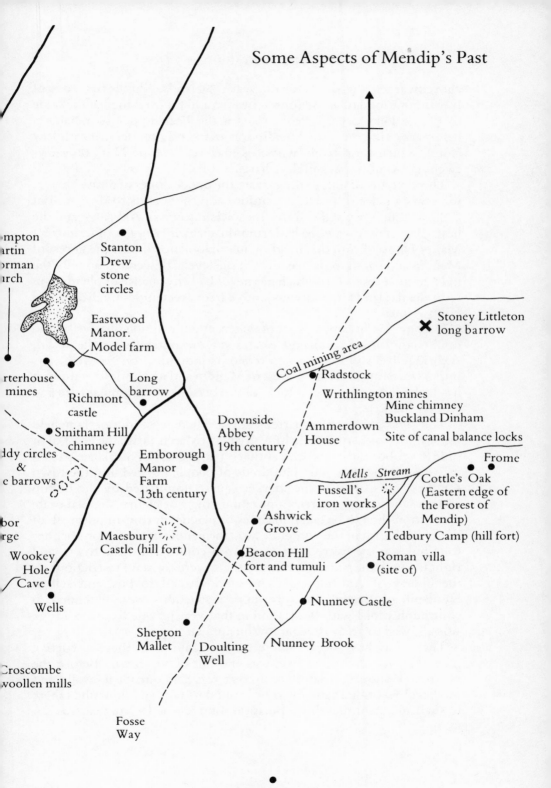

Some Aspects of Mendip's Past

mpton
artin
orman
rch

Stanton
Drew
stone
circles

Eastwood
Manor.
Model farm

rterhouse
mines

Richmont
castle

Long
barrow

Smitham Hill
chimney

ddy circles
&
e barrows

Emborough
Manor
Farm
13th century

bor
rge

Wookey
Hole
Cave

Wells

Maesbury
Castle (hill fort)

Croscombe
woollen mills

Shepton
Mallet

Doulting
Well

Fosse
Way

Downside
Abbey
19th century

Ashwick
Grove

Beacon Hill
fort and tumuli

Nunney Brook

Coal mining area

Radstock

Writhlington mines

Ammerdown
House

Mells Stream

Fussell's
iron works

✕ Stoney Littleton
long barrow

Mine chimney
Buckland Dinham

Site of canal balance locks

Frome

Cottle's Oak
(Eastern edge of
the Forest of
Mendip)

Tedbury Camp (hill fort)

Roman villa
(site of)

Nunney Castle

Site of Witham Friary

churchwarden's accounts for the year 1580 reads: "Pd the firste day of July for one lood of wood for the Beaken and for carryinge of the same to Croke Peke 0.5.0." From the sea the Peak is not so reliable a landmark. Like much of Mendip it is frequently hidden beneath low cloud, which is probably why it is marked "See me Not" on early-twentieth-century Admiralty charts.

The next line of hills to the east are the upper slopes of Shute Shelve, for years a place of public execution, and the woods to the south of Callow Hill. They stand above the ancient town of Axbridge and the best view of them is to be had from the elegant *belvedere* of its ancient Manor House. From that height you can look north over the Forest of Mendip and south to the pastures of the levels, desecrated now by the ugly circular reservoir, which has never had any chance of blending in with the flat landscape, divided into narrow rectangles by droves and willow-lined drainage rhynes.

Despite that unhappy sheet of water, and the unimaginative but no doubt comfortable housing estates on the outskirts of the town, Axbridge has still managed to retain its individuality. As well as its importance for the Saxon Forest of Mendip and its Domesday mint, it has had a long history as a local centre because of its annual fairs and weekly markets.

The fairs dated from a charter of 1239. There were four of them held on St Barnabas Day (June 4th); Lady Day (March 25th); the Feast of St Jude (October 28th); and on February 3rd, the day of St Blaize, patron of weavers and clothiers. Hundreds of people flocked into the town for these fairs, held in the market square dominated by the hilltop church whose tower carries a puzzling effigy of Henry VI. Elaborate precautions had to be taken in times of plague; during an outbreak of the Black Death in the winter of 1500 the people of Compton Bishop, four miles away, were prevented from coming into the town, and right through the sixteenth century there were constant restrictions on the liberty of Axbridge citizens who wanted to buy and sell in Huntspill or Bristol. In 1593 those restrictions were extended to communications with Wells, and in that year no one from Axbridge was allowed to go to Binegar's Whitsun Fair.

There may have been some economic gain from these restrictive measures, for Axbridge Fair was the life of the town. Before the Norman Conquest a Saturday market was held outside its walls, but medieval Axbridge actually grew around its fair, and flourished there to such an extent that the population soon reached a size that was not exceeded until the 1970s. Each of the 32 burgesses of the town had a free stall at the fairs, and these could be inherited by their widows.

In the tenth century, Axbridge was a fortified town surrounded by a wall about a third of a mile in length, and it is still justifiably aware of its past. Its fine local history museum is housed in a sixteenth-century building, which once consisted of four shops with room for storage and accommodation above them. A circular walk from there takes you out of that commercial heart of the town (now a spacious and elegant square), down Moorland Street, where the shambles have been converted into bijoux dwellings, and on to the pastures of the levels, which were once the town allotments. There were originally 32 of them, one for each of the burgesses. Fifteen of them still remained at the time of the First World War, when army mules were pastured here. The boundaries were marked out by stones or by the rhynes which were cut when draining got under way here in the early nineteenth century. Now the rhynes and droves survive, but the allotments have been sold off to local farms.

The way back to the centre of the town goes past the burgesses' houses on West Street and the late-seventeenth-century manor house. When that was being built the curfew bell installed by the Normans was still rung in the town. It was still heard up to 1870 when Axbridge got its first gas lights, but few people were quite sure why. One elderly citizen told Frank Knight, at the turn of the century, that "Curfey" was rung to guide people to church on foggy nights.

The Saxon burgh of Axbridge has always been linked somewhat uneasily with its companion town of Cheddar, where Saxon kings appear to have built at least three successive palaces. The site of the most recent one, together with its corn mill, has been marked out on the grass outside the Kings of Wessex school. Alfred had a palace here, where the Saxon witan was regularly held, but the last timber building to be put up on the site was built by his grandson, Athelstan, in the tenth century. On a piece of higher ground beside the short concrete pillars that mark out the area of his palace are the remains of the fourteenth-century chapel of St Columbanus, the seventh-century founder of monasteries and disciple of Gildas.

Now all that remains of Cheddar's Saxon and Norman past is a corbel on the south-east corner of the sanctuary in the church. Even Pay Street, whose name is believed to be a corruption of Palais Street, was changed to Station Road when the railway came in 1869. The passer-by will not see any signs of medieval Cheddar apart from the fine butter cross, its steps worn by generations of traders, and whose pillars and canopy were carefully restored in 1887. Yet traces of very old buildings do still exist in the town, although they are mostly hidden by later façades. In May 1983, a house in North Street had a last-minute reprieve from the bulldozers, when it was discovered that part of its interior dated from the fourteenth century.

By the eighteenth century royal Cheddar had completely degenerated. Wilberforce found it a place with "no dawn of comfort either spiritual or temporal" and he promised Hannah More that he would finance any attempt she could make to better the wretched lot of its people. Cheddar's housing reflected the town's poverty well into the twentieth century. At the time of the First World War the squatters' houses (built by the roadside in a single day) had only just been pulled down. They had once lined the Lippiatt to the east of the town, along the lane which led to the hillside grazing. Now the best of Cheddar lies in the stone cottages of Redcliffe Street and in those to the west of the Gorge round the former mill ponds fed by the waters of the underground rivers.

Like most towns, Cheddar has many personalities. Three predominate: the old town which has belonged for centuries to farmers, miners and quarrymen; the new housing for people who do not have to live on top of their work; and the tourist strip. Most of the latter is concentrated at the lower end of the Gorge, although it extends upwards as far as the show caves. These defy vulgarization, but it is much pleasanter to visit them on a cold day out of season when you may be lucky enough to get them completely to yourself. Then it is possible to be grateful for the lighting which reveals the delicate, infinitely slowly growing rock formations and the contrasting colours of the differing metals and chemicals in the stone.

These caves have been on show to the public since the mid-nineteenth century, but Cheddar Gorge was an objective for tourists long before then. In 1150, Henry of Huntingdon described it as one of the four wonders of England, and throughout the centuries the Somerset gentry have driven to Cheddar to show their visitors the marvels of the cliffs.

The caves, which were used as a storehouse for valuable stained glass during the last war, belong to the vast amusement industry that Lord Bath has made out of his Longleat estate. So the coaches and cars of his customers go half way up the Gorge spilling their contents into the tourist junk shops, the amusement arcades, the cafés and the caves.

It is not all horrid. Someone has imaginatively planted a garden of sweet-smelling shrubs for the blind beside Cheddar waters; and it is from a well laid out and informative museum that the skeleton of Cheddar man, some thousands of years younger than the people who hunted with the Westbury flints, grins at the holiday families.

The more adventurous and strong-winded climb the steps to the look-out point at Jacob's Tower, a folly resembling an inland lighthouse, built by an eccentric miller of Cheddar, who finally went completely mad and tried to fly across the Gorge. From there they can see the whole of the Somerset levels laid out before them like a geography lesson in a sand tray. Others may wander up the Gorge itself, bravely leaving the shelter of cars and coaches to gaze at rock climbers negotiating the near-impossible overhangs of rock.

The climbers are answering man's fundamental need to pit himself against nature; and for all its commercialization the elements will always be an ever-present factor in the Gorge. The road often has to be closed to traffic because of some natural upheaval. After the violent thunderstorms and torrential rain of July 12th 1982, the electronic sensors which had been fixed to a potentially dangerous rock registered an imminent fall. Cars were not allowed by until it had been safely dislodged by a team from Bovis engineers led by Chris Bradshaw. From time to time proposals have been made that the Gorge should be closed to traffic. That would enable people to enjoy the spectacular scenery in peace, but naturally the traders strongly oppose such an idea, while the town officials are seriously worried about parking provision. As things stand the National Trust together with the Somerset Trust for Nature Conservation are saving the upper reaches of the Gorge and protecting the wildlife of the rocks.

It is impossible to leave Cheddar without mentioning cheese, although for a long time cheese straws have been the only cheese products to be manufactured in the town. The nearest place at which Cheddar cheese is now actually made is Chewton Mendip, several miles to the north-east.

Although the special Somerset cheese has taken the name of Cheddar, it was once made on almost every farm on Mendip. Cheese was part of the dairy economy, and its making was an essential part of the work of a farmer's wife. In fact it was so important that any girl who could make a good cheese could take her pick of farming husbands. To that end many parents found it a good investment to apprentice their daughters to farmers' wives renowned for their skill, or to send them to a cheese-making school such as the one that was set up in Wells at the Palace Farm in 1889.

The school was set up by a committee belonging to the Bath and West Society, who purchased the whole of the milk yield from the herd belonging to Mr C. E. Wickham, who was the Bishop's tenant at that time. Mr Wickham's other task was to provide board and lodging for some of the students attending the school and for their teacher. She was the daughter of Mr H. Cannon of Milton Clevedon near Evercreech, who according to the committee's report on the venture enjoyed "a reputation second to none as a maker of Cheddar Cheese". The course lasted for four weeks and the fee, which included board, lodging and tuition, came to eight guineas.

The Bath and West Society became seriously interested in cheese making in the mid-nineteenth century, when the chemist Augustus Voelcker started working as a consultant in a voluntary capacity. His main innovation was to recommend the use of thermometers to register the temperature of the milk when it was ready for the rennet to be added. He claimed they were "invaluable tools" and that their use was a great improvement on the old method of allowing the dairy maids to be guided entirely by their own feelings, which were necessarily as "variable as those of other mortals".

Nearer home to Cheddar than the cheese are the market gardens that line the road to the east as far as the village of Rodney Stoke. They climb up the hills as far as the rocks so that the whole slope glistens like water with the polythene which protects the young plants in spring. This sheltered ground is the garden of Mendip and has been so many years. In the seventeenth century Axbridge church steps were reserved for the sale of the soft fruit and vegetables produced here; and in the nineteenth the vegetable producers of the Cheddar Valley took their goods to Bristol in flat-bottomed carts, like those made by John Kerslake, Winscombe's wheelwright, carpenter and undertaker at that time. In 1869 the railway went along the Cheddar Valley to Wells and took so much fruit to market that the track became known as the strawberry line. Now the produce goes by van as far as London and the other main cities in the south, and the land on which it grows fetches up to £4000 an acre.

Strawberries are still one of the main crops of these market gardens, and for decades they were far and away the most important. Their massive cultivation began about a hundred years ago with the cultivation of Royal Sovereigns, later to be replaced by the Cambridge varieties which are less susceptible to disease. When the industry started heather and bracken from Blackdown was arranged round the plants to keep the ripening fruit from the mud, then Sparta grass from the local paper mill was used for that purpose before a return to the straw which initially gave the fruit its English name. Now, ripening under cloches, the fruit is protected by a carpet of black polythene.

Strawberry growing is still a family affair. There is no large, impersonal company ranching these fields; and in the busy times of the year, during the July and August planting and the late-spring picking all the members of the family turn to, and casual labour is hired from Wells, Cheddar and the surrounding villages. Cheddar Vale strawberry growers only go in for Pick Your Own when the best of the crop has been sent to the national markets, and even then they seem to prefer to sell punnets to passing motorists from the roadside. Although the era of the tasteless all-the-year-round strawberry is now with us, the growers of Cheddar Valley persist in producing luscious fruit in due season. But the acreage given over to strawberries continues to decline, and many strawberry growers have had to take up industrial work with E.M.I., while the gardens are turned over to less labour-intensive crops.

Draycott village in the heart of the market gardens still calls its festival week a strawberry fair, and the pub by the old railway station there, like the one at the terminus at Wells, is still known as the Strawberry Special. But Cheddar strawberries are no longer sold in Wells market square, although that city is still the natural conclusion of any exploration of this part of Mendip.

Wells is a place that people love. In the fourteenth century it was the largest town in Somerset, having some nine hundred inhabitants. Now that number has been increased more than tenfold, and most of the people who live in and around the city are not Somerset. Many of these newcomers take on the affection that Wells' birthright citizens have always felt for the place. I am happy that when I could choose to live anywhere in England, I settled in Priest Row, opposite the city church of St Cuthbert, in the road where, in the 1920s, Herbert Balch, Wells' postmaster and first citizen, lived with all his geological treasures until he moved into the premises of the museum he founded. When in 1931 he retired from the Post Office, but not from his work as local historian and exponent of natural history, he declared: "Wells is my home and my life, and the only place in the world for me. It has a real vital interest for me and I can always see work waiting to be done."

Balch was one of the first men to make a systematic exploration of Mendip's caves; he inaugurated the Wells Museum, housed on the cathedral green; and, among his many minor but valuable pieces of work, he restored the domed circular buddle house by the stream in wooded Biddlecombe below the main Wells to Bristol road. It makes the goal of many enchanting walks from the edge of the hillside village of West Horrington.

To reach that village from Wells, you must go along St Thomas's Street to the north of the cathedral. It was there that Balch was born, on November 4th 1869. Its stone cottages and mazes of courtyards make it one of the most fascinating streets in a city that is full of unexpected ways. Part of its romance stems cruelly from the fact that it was once the poorest area in the city. At the beginning of the nineteenth century it was known as Turkey, probably because of the heathenish nature of its inhabitants, who were so independent of the rest of Wells that they elected their own mayor. The present church was built half way up the street in an attempt to provide an oasis of reform. Now the families for whom it was first intended have died out or moved on, and their homes have mostly been gentrified. It would be foolish to scorn that, for the alternative is demolition.

Balch died on May 27th 1958, and his mantle fell to Dr R. D. Reid, scientist by profession and Wells historian by accident of birth and inclination who died on December 27th 1983 at the age of eighty-five. In his retirement he lived in the house he had known since childhood, and which he claimed to be the oldest in Wells. Its heart is a fourteenth-century hall encased in stylish additions of three or four hundred years later. It stands in a street where the wealthy families of the city of Wells once used to live, and which still retains something of the elegance it must have had when lime trees grew down its centre, even though it is now part of a one-way race-track round the city.

From that place, Dr Reid, always generous with his time to anybody who shared his interest in the story of both cathedral and city, started off on his walks round Wells. Each one led to a lively encounter with the past. Indeed it is impossible to live exclusively in the present in Wells, although the inexorable streams of heavy traffic make it equally impossible to ignore the city's involvement with the pressures of the present. Fortunately the city is still small enough to be a place where people walk. Crowds of visitors to the cathedral throng the pavements, alongside gutters running with the waters from the wells in the garden of the Bishop's Palace. By six o'clock the tourist-pilgrims have gone, for the motorways have badly hit Wells' old bed-and-breakfast trade. In the evenings and during the winter months the real life of the city emerges, upheld by the cathedral, its attached music school, and the events that cluster round the Blue School, a large and modern comprehensive which still has links with its seventeenth-century beginnings, when it was attended by some of the cleverer sons of the Priddy miners.

CHAPTER IX

East of Wells: Sacrifice Area

To THE EAST of Wells, the character of Mendip changes completely. As the planners have not seen fit to label any of it as being an area of "outstanding natural beauty", the wooded hills and the steep valleys that lie within the triangle of roads linking the towns of Shepton Mallet, Frome and Radstock are left to the mercy of the quarry owners and developers. Certainly this is a less immediately spectactular landscape than the heights of Crook Peak, Shute Shelve and Blackdown to the west, but it holds even more surprises in the folds of its valleys than those bare uplands can achieve. Walking here, I have often felt myself to be quite remote from habitation, and illusionary as this feeling is (the nearest farm building is never more than a mile or so away and a main road can well be closer) I am none the less grateful for the effect of a gently cultivated wilderness, and all the more angry when I find it wrecked by a quarry.

The desecration that the stone men have made here is apparent as soon as you leave Wells, whether you drive beneath Tor Woods to the village of Dulcote, or turn your back on the cathedral and walk along the field path that goes through Bishop's meadows. To the right is Dulcote hill, or rather the façade of Dulcote hill, for behind the thin edge of rock above the road, a whole hill has been eaten away. Past that, the quarries can be forgotten until you reach the other side of Shepton Mallet. The first village you reach is Croscombe, and ironically if its buildings please you — and I cannot imagine who would not delight in them — then it is largely because they are made of local stone.

On the old road along the Croscombe hillside, which is now used for taking fodder to the cattle, many of the poorer people clacked their needles as they made their way to the fairs of Shepton, Glastonbury, Wells, Cheddar and Axbridge. Knitting helped to supplement the money on which the poorest families struggled to live, and both men and women took it up as a full- or part-time occupation. Knitters, who were marked down as such on the early census returns, may have been on the bread line, but the hosiery manufacturers, such as William Urch, who flourished at nearby Nettlebridge in the late 1870s, were men of substance, and at the beginning of the nineteenth century, Shepton Mallet was renowned as a centre for "fine knit hose".

Hose were an essential commodity, but their manufacture was always of less account than that of woven goods. It was in cloth that the large fortunes were to be made and both Shepton Mallet and Frome were notable cloth towns. The last mill in Shepton closed in 1930, but by that time it was silk and crêpe rather than woollen broad cloth that was being turned out.

At the culmination of its prosperity in the late eighteenth century, Frome produced 150,000 yards of cloth annually, and John Billingsley reported that its mills provided employment for more than one third of its population of seventeen hundred families.

Nearly a hundred years before that, Daniel Defoe reckoned that the town had more inhabitants than Bath or Salisbury, and he concluded that if the cloth trade continued to increase at the rate it had done for the past twenty or thirty years, Frome could be "one of the greatest and wealthiest inland towns in England". His prophecy came true, and the wealth brought elegance and culture. The great house of the Champneys at Orchardleigh to the north of the town rivalled Marston Bigot to the south. The rich turned to charity, and the Blue House with its school and home for old women of the parish was established.

At this time in the town's history, Elizabeth Rowe, poetess and friend of the saintly Bishop Ken, was devoting herself to literature and piety. She was born in Ilchester in 1674, the daughter of Walter Singer, a wealthy wool merchant. Her work was nationally acclaimed in literary circles, and in her mid-thirties it led her to marry an admirer, Nicholas Rowe, a classical scholar and fourteen years her junior. They settled in Egford, her poems giving evidence of an idyllically happy union. Alas, it only lasted five years. Nicholas died in 1715, and Elizabeth returned to her father's house to live and write in Frome.

The crash came to the town in the early nineteenth century, as the cotton mills of the north of England took away the trade from the woollen mills of the south. On September 1st 1825 William Cobbett rode into the town from neighbouring Warminster. He was shocked to find two or three hundred unemployed weavers cracking stones on the roadside for a living.

It was then that Frome began to fall into a state of decay, and it is only owing to the energy, enterprise and constant vigilance of the post-war voluntary preservation society that any of the town's eighteenth- century splendour has been saved and restored. When that society appealed for funds to rebuild the Blue School itself, and to reinstate it as an almshouse, Sir John Betjeman blessed the project. He took the opportunity to make a general observation: "Indeed the time is soon coming when people will discover that old towns and motor-cars are incompatible . . . you can't really appreciate an historic town like Frome without walking about in it on foot."

Frome is indeed a good example of that point. It gives nothing away at all to the passing motorist; to find its heart you must walk through its narrow cobbled back streets, climb the hill behind the George Inn to the high pavement where the small shops are, or go north along the crumbling elegance of Vallis Way to Milk Street where fine but disintegrating, eighteenth-century houses are encircled by the new housing estates.

Shepton Mallet is smaller, but again it will tell you nothing along its through roads, and not much from the shops and alleys of its pedestrian centre. To get to know it you must explore as far as Darshill, the village behind the site where the old silk mill stood on the Croscombe side. That is a good place to live now, despite the sewage works that have replaced the mill, but the wretched conditions that the weavers' families had to put up with are still evident. The shells of some of their homes are still there, the rock of the hillside serving as a back wall. These ruins make a sad contrast with the prettily restored and comfortable cottages that stand beside them.

Two hundred years ago, when the poor lived in Darshill, the rich lived further up the hill nearer to the centre of Shepton and Bowlish, where one elegant mansion is now open to the public as an expense-account eating place. But the best buildings are to be found in the maze of lanes and courtyards that fill the valley beneath the town, and a walk there is especially good in summer when the mellowed yellow stone of the long dead well-to-do merchants' houses is covered in a lively profusion of flowering climbers.

Shepton Mallet's more modest prosperity outlived that of Frome because the town had a major secondary industry in brewing and cider making. This has continued although the original producers of beer and cider have now been drowned out in the perry of Showering's Babycham, whose cute plaster Bambi does nothing to enhance the eastern approach to the town. The creature is the symbol of a local monopoly, for the Anglo Apple Mills which used to produce Mendip Apple Nectar at Darshill went out of business in 1979.

It was in 1858 that the Shepton breweries gave the town its special prominence in the drinks trade. In that year, Mr William Clarke, who had set up a brewery in the town, discovered that the product of the Shepton Mallet Water Company, and particularly that from the Mill Pond Spring at Windsor's Hill, made a very good beer. In 1864 the Anglo-Bavarian brewery was set up, and its buildings, put to other uses now, dominate the entrance to the town from Wells. In its early days a donkey engine pump from the Radstock coal mines was used to get the water up to the brewery.

The town of Shepton is now almost synonymous with Showerings which have even taken over the old railway viaduct and incorporated it into the garden beside the factory. The firm, which amalgamated with R. N. Coates, the cider makers of Nailsea, in 1956, and is now part of Allied-Lyons P.L.C., evolved its pear drink in 1953 to a formula devised by Francis Showering and his three brothers. As shoemakers and hoteliers, the Showerings were prominent in Shepton Mallet long before they started up their brewery in Kilver Street in the late eighteenth century. The firm they set up now employs more than eight hundred people in the area, some of whom work at the Coates Gaynor bottling site close to the old Charlton Brewery, which with its massive stabling and crumbling manager's house, awaits demolition or total decay at the point where the green lane of the Roman Fosse Way meets the old toll road to Frome.

Radstock, the third town of the triangle, has long owed its living to coal, although the Mendip coal measures, and hence the sites of the old collieries spread nearly as far south-west as Oakhill. Moorewood colliery at Ashwick just outside that village did not close down until 1933, although by that time most mining was centred round Radstock and its close neighbour, Midsomer Norton.

Radstock, which Pevsner found "really desperately ugly" but which Iain Nairn considered "fascinating", was dominated by its coal mines for two hundred years. The smartly painted winching gear, set up in the centre of the town, is the one deliberate memorial to its place in British mining history. The batches which still form pyramids of slag heaps on the skyline will soon look like natural hills as the vegetation rapidly takes over; and the remains of the old mine workings above ground are all being put to other uses. For the town which grew rapidly on its coal during the latter part of the nineteenth century, has turned its back on an industry which once employed over seven thousand people. The terraces of miners' cottages, built by the Waldegraves for their workers long before the National Coal Board took over the mines, stand as a reminder of the reason for Radstock's growth. Their insistent presence clothes the valley in which the town was built.

Now that the east Mendip cloth trade is over and the mines have all been closed down, the biggest source of employment in the area, after the quarries, is the print industry. Many families in Radstock and Midsomer Norton are dependent on the fortunes of the British Printing Corporation, which is based there and which has a packaging site on Norton Hill where the largest of the Somerset collieries once operated. In Frome the firm of Butler and Tanner gives work to some four hundred people, who follow a most honourable local tradition. For the town was the birthplace of the much-prized Victorian Daniel Press, whose publications are still keenly collected. Its founder, C. H. O. Daniel, was the vicar's son and learnt to print as a young boy in 1845, setting texts for his father's sermons on a parlour press. His example of successful and elegant home printing has been followed in the 1980s by Graeme Baresford Young, who prints and publishes under the sign of Bran's Head, from one of the rambling old houses in Milk Street.

In winter the young Daniel set his type by the aid of a gas light whose holder was shaped locally at Cockeys' iron foundry. That firm grew out of the seventeenth-century bell foundry from which Bell Lane got its name, and which cast the bells for the neighbouring churches of Nunney, Wanstrow and Whatley. The Cockeys had one serious rival in the Bilbies of Chew Stoke to the west, but their bells hang together at Kilmersdon, a church which also includes some work from the foundry of J. W. Singer, which produced ornamental church metal work throughout the nineteenth century.

These east Mendip villages are ensconced in rich farmland. In value it competes with the fertile northern lowlands between the heights of the true Mendip ridge and the hills around Wrington. And although the ridge between Shepton Mallet and Frome is full of surface limestone, its slopes can be twice as costly as those in the west. For the most part, good land has made good farmers like the Hendy family of Faulkland.

Mrs Hendy has lived at Upper Row farm all her life. Her family moved into the hills from Wedmore in 1900, and her husband took over the farm during the last war. At that time he was milking 25 to 30 shorthorns and growing 40 to 50 acres of flax on government contract for parachute-making in Devizes. It was a hard crop to manage, for although it takes only a hundred days from sowing to harvest, it has to be pulled by hand. It would have been an almost impossible task without the labour of Italian prisoners of war.

Being brought up on the land may involve working beneath it. This is a region where for a long time mining and farming went closely together, and to a more limited extent that now holds true for the quarries. Mr Hendy's neighbour, Ted Green of Horsepond Farm in Faulkland, is the son of a miner who was determined not to let his children go down the pit. Mr Green has been farming for over 40 years now, and for the latter half of that time he has kept a large pedigree Jersey dairy herd.

This is the countryside that John Billingsley, the leader of agricultural improvement in the late eighteenth century, knew well. You can reach the ruins of his house at Ashwick Grove, which was demolished as recently as 1955, by following the old carriage way from St Dunstan's well at Stoke Bottom. Now it is completely grassed over and part of the hillside field, but the levelled stretch round the contour marks out the drive along which he and his agents came to supervise the mill he was so glad to get rid of.

At present it is a quiet way, for not only has the mill long since disappeared, but the quarry at its western end is no longer working. It is a peace that could be shattered if the quarry were ever to be restarted or if the Fairy Cave, which is entered from that site, should be opened to the public. In the peace the place enjoys now, deer graze in the wood across the lane, and can jump out in the path of the walker bound for Billingsley's ghost. His driveway first skirts the wood, and then follows the stream that runs through it, an idyllic place whose romance is not dispelled by the scent of crushed garlic as you walk over the white ramsons that carpet it. On its way to the house the drive passes a simple folly, a little temple-shaped sun house carved out of the rock. It is a modest pleasure place compared to the elaborate grottoes that the Fussells later devised round the lake they made beneath their house at Chantry.

However, Ashwick Grove can boast one real antiquity. The main drive from the front of the house is the Roman Fosse Way leading up to Beacon Hill. Mr Perkins of Oakhill must have driven down that avenue when he was summoned to help Billingsley prepare his report on the state of farming in Somerset for the newly formed Board of Agriculture. It would be nice to think that these two gentlemen consulted one of the best of their contemporary farmers in the district, even though she was a woman. Jane Folliott settled in Nunney in 1790, and managed her land so successfully that when she died 26 years later she left the respectable fortune of £3000.

Billingsley's successor in eastern Mendip now is Lord Hylton of Ammerdown. His pioneering takes the welcome form of a return to a scientifically tested routine of organic farming based on a four-year rotation, which gives the land a chance to renew itself naturally; and he has set up a grain syndicate where the local farmers can make their own cattle feed before selling the surplus.

The wooded hill of Ammerdown looks over the village of Kilmersdon, where the Jollifes, Lord Hylton's family, lived until 1770, and which is still very much part of his estate. Half of Kilmersdon's three hundred inhabitants are tenants of the district housing association, which he set up when such an arrangement was made possible by the 1974 Act. It is a village with a conscious identity that has been partly fostered by investigations for a survey carried out through the Hugh of Witham Foundation. The actual work was organized, and the final report compiled, by the architect Roger Kelly and his wife Maritsa, who were anxious to see how this village, with its single combined shop and post office and no village hall, could extend its community life and enterprises.

While they were doing that work, the Kellys were themselves tenants of Lord Hylton, living at Orange Tree Farm, one of the oldest houses in a village where most of the buildings date from the eighteenth century. Before they came to Kilmersdon, the low rambling house, set sideways to the road, was the home of Mr Coles, the retired village school master, who lived well into his eighties, and employed himself in his old age by keeping bees and poultry. Many good gardeners around learnt their skills from him.

The school in which he taught stands on the top of a hill that shares with Greenwich Hill the distinction of having been acclaimed as the one Jack and Jill climbed to fetch their pail of water. Whether they did have that adventure here or not, they would have found no school on the hill or in the village, rhyming "water" with "after" would not have been possible after the seventeenth century, and it was not until 1707 that Kilmersdon had a school at all. That first school house, also

Above: Wells Cathedral from the Bishop's Meadows

Below left: Vicars Close, Wells; the fourteenth–century houses of the Vicars Choral. *Below right:* The Norman pillars of Compton Martin Church

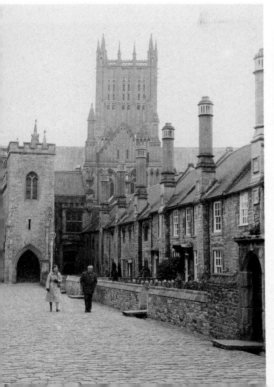

Above left and right: Stone heads at the south door of
Compton Martin Church

Mendip people. *Below left:* Ernie Small with truckles of Cheddar
Cheese in the 1940s. *Below right:* Hannah More: the good angel of
Shipham, Rowberrow and Cheddar

FROM A PORTRAIT OF MRS HANNAH MORE. By Singleton
BEQUEATHED BY SIR ROBERT INGLIS, BART. M.P.
TO SIR T. D. ACKLAND, BART. IN THE YEAR 1855

Mendip people. *Above:* Richard Cox Gough, discoverer of the most famous show cave in Cheddar Gorge, with some of his large family

Below: The floods at Cheddar Gorge, 1968

Above: The bridge at Chew Stoke
Left: A lead miner's buddlehouse in Biddlecombe, West Horrington
Below: Emborough Manor; part of this farmhouse dates from the thirteenth century, making it the oldest house on Mendip.

Above: Mill
workers' cottages
built into the side
of the hill
at Darshill,
Shepton Mallet

Above: Water from the Sheppy
channelled to form part of
the ornamental landscaping
of Dinder village
Right: One of Fussell's
Italianate grottos by his
pleasure lake at Chantry

Above: The gentle face of Mendip; the southern slope at Axbridge

Below: Where the millennia meet; the ancient seabed separating the dolomitic and conglomerate limestone at Vallis Vale, Frome

Above and below: Coppicing in the Somerset Trust for Nature Conservation's reserve at Asham Wood

Underneath the hills: cavers in G.B. Cavern, Charterhouse, gaze at
the pure white stalactites hanging from the roof

inhabited by one of Lord Hylton's tenants, is a stone building of modest charm, standing at the bottom of the hill by the church and the Jollife Arms. Beside it, a footpath across the stream climbs to the railway line, which once linked the villagers with Bath and Radstock. Now they have to wait for infrequent buses, little comforted by the fact that the bus shelter is the old village lock-up, beautifully restored and preserved.

On the other side of Ammerdown Park is the forsaken village of Hardington, the home of the Bampfyldes from the sixteenth to the nineteenth centuries. The founder of the family fortune was that ruthless encloser of lands whom John Leland commented on so sharply. Extensive enclosures also went on when the Knatchbulls emparked Babington to the south of Ammerdown. No trace of that village remains. The great house stands quite alone, with an eighteenth-century church of the most elegant proportions on its front lawn.

The Horners are the fourth great family on this side of Mendip. The village of Mells owes much of its present-day charm to the pertinacity of the early members of that family in adding to their acres by fair deeds and foul; and to the way their successors, despite continual wrangles over the industrial projects of the Fussells, achieved a reputation for holding court with elegance and erudition. The Lady Horner of the first years of this century was one of the "souls", a great patron of the arts and a hostess to Balfour and Asquith.

The learning was spread to the villagers. A grammar school was established in Mells in 1524; and in the early seventeenth century the Church House was turned into an additional school. Later a reading room for adults was set up near the mill, deserted now, but once a centre of village activity. There is still a public consciousness about Mells. It is a village of flowers. In February the lanes and banks are white with snowdrops, while so many daffodils have been planted here that a festival to celebrate them is held each April.

Yet it is a scattered village, and it is easy for the casual visitor to miss the best parts of it. In the fifteenth century Abbot John de Selwood of Glastonbury had the pleasing idea of building it in the shape of a cross with the church at the centre, but only the southern arm, the present New Street, was built. The rest of the village grew later, around the stream to the south-east. So now most visitors feel that they have seen Mells, once they have walked down Selwood's short street (much rebuilt since his time), found the Burne-Jones peacock panel and the

Munnings equestrian statue in the church, and glimpsed the roofs of the Tudor manor house where Ronald Knox spent his retirement.

Like most others on eastern Mendip, the people of Mells relied on mining and weaving to support their families. The decline of the cloth trade in the eighteenth and nineteenth centuries caused poverty as dire as that which Cobbett found in Frome, save that in a more rural area there were more opportunities to stave off hunger by poaching. It was not a palliative that the Horners condoned; as many men were transported from Mells as from any other comparable village.

Mells was a rigidly feudal village, although its rulers could be benevolent. The Horners' interest in education continued. In 1830 a school was set up in disused weavers' premises, but there was no intention that learning should ever upset the hierarchy. At election time the squire rode into Wells, his tenants behind him, under threat of receiving notice to quit if they did not vote for the Tory candidate.

In the 1820s, when the industrial Fussells were ready to make their mark as landed gentry, they planted trees in three separate areas so as to discover which had the best soil. The lot fell to land which may have belonged to the fourteenth-century chantry chapel in Whatley church. It was a happy choice, for the ground stood on a ridge to the south of Mells, above the stream later to be landscaped into a lake with a carriage drive all around it. Those waters powered another of the Fussell mills.

There James Fussell (the fifth of that name) built his family house in 1825 and set up the village of Chantry, still obstinately known by some of its inhabitants as Little Elm (Great Elm lies to the east of Mells) as the notice above the White Horse inn signifies. Beside the house he built a church, marking the base of its minute spire with an angel bearing a sickle, one of the family's own edge tool products.

The memory of the Fussells will never leave Chantry. Arthur Perry, who was church organist there to the late 1970s and one of the village's oldest inhabitants, claimed that James's ghost haunts the lake. It would be a good choice for any spirit to visit. The lake James created is beautiful once again: though not so many years ago its waters were desperately polluted with oil from the quarry works above it. Lake and house are in private hands, but through the Somerset Trust for Nature Conservation it is possible for parties of visitors to go there. It is a good place to be at any time of the year but especially so in spring when the woods around it abound in anemones and primroses, and you may see a pair of nesting dippers skimming the surface of the lake and proving the renewed purity of its waters.

The village of Nunney, which boasts the only remaining ruins of a medieval castle on Mendip, lies in the next valley to the south. The wool trade flourished in this village too, and among Nunney's most prominent inhabitants in the seventeenth century were the Flower family, whose members were both wealthy clothiers and leading Nonconformists.

There are still signs of the place where the wool was washed by the river which flows behind the main street; but it is the castle, really no more than a crenellated manor house, that attracts the visitors. Sir John de la Mare was licensed to fortify his home by Edward III in 1373. There it stood defending the roads through the hills until it was slighted in 1645, after Colonel Richard Prater who had held it with 80 men was forced to surrender to Cromwell's army. Only the shell of the building, with its four battered towers, remain, but at least it is saved the indignity which it suffered early in the nineteenth century when it was used as a kennel for hounds.

It stands in a beautiful setting, as the builders of the new manor house, which was built beside it in the eighteenth century, surely appreciated, but it must have been obvious to the most obtuse of military strategists that a castle built in the dip of the hills was unlikely to survive in the age of gunpowder. Yet the land around Nunney had been fought over long before that invention. In 1860, 250 ancient British gold and silver coins were found in a field belonging to Westdown Farm, and such a large hoard is usually taken to indicate the place of a tribal boundary. In this case the skirmishes would have been between the Dobunni whose territory extended as far north as the Cotswolds, and the Durotoniges whose lands went south into Dorset.

The Romans were here too. A villa of the fourth century AD was discovered in 1837 above Whatley Combe to the north of the village. A Mr Shore, who owned the land at that time, tried to protect the mosaic of its pavement with a covering shed, but that did not prevent its destruction by nineteenth-century vandals, sightseers snatching souvenirs, and of course the Mendip weather. Luckily somebody had the foresight to make a drawing of the pavement which shows Orpheus and his lyre taming the wild beasts. It is now in the local history museum at Frome.

Nunney was settled so early because it stands at the junction of several natural highways. It is quite possible that the Saxon king, Cenwalh, made this his headquarters in his campaigns against the Celts, in the middle of the seventh century. It could well have been from here that he rode south to victory, for the Battle of Posentesbyrig in 661 is thought to have taken place on Postlebury Hill. Evidence of a Celtic settlement has been found there, among the clay pits by the abandoned farm.

Postlebury Wood, with its deer and badgers, lies between the villages of Trudox Hill and Witham Friary on the edge of Selwood Forest. Although the geological purists cannot allow the area around Postlebury Hill (which is higher than Crook Peak to the west) to be part of Mendip, it has played such an important role in the history of the region that it must be included. The Royal Hunting Forest of Selwood once reached almost to the eastern edge of the Forest of Mendip, St Dunstan's Well at Stoke Bottom was recorded in an eighteenth-century perambulation as one of the boundary marks, and a thirteenth-century document suggests that there was a Saxon palace at Frome comparable to that of Cheddar.

Here also the existence of the hunting forest caused friction between church and monarch. At Witham, St Hugh had no sympathy for the forest and its special laws, and he was angry at the way the foresters harassed the poor country people. He picked on the Latin derivation of the word forester (*foris stare*, to stand outside) to declare: "Yes, that is the right name for them, for they will remain outside the kingdom of God."

Postlebury itself was not originally part of the Royal Forest, but it was encroached upon by the king's foresters, and in 1258 a William de Postlebri with two companions was fined for poaching there. About that time Henry de Montfort of Nunney, a kinsman of the Simon who founded the English Parliament, was one of the verderers, but his sympathies appear to have lain with church and commoners. In 1261, when members of the household of Witham Friary entered the forest and killed a doe, their nets were discovered and handed to Henry, who was careless enough to lose them to the original poachers.

The Forest of Mendip extended to Cottle's Ash, now Cottle's Oak, an uninteresting suburb to the north-west of Frome. A little to the north of that the coal measures start, and the relics of the coal mines punctuate the landscape, starting with the brick chimney of Buckland Dinham, in a field beside the road between Frome and Radstock.

About three miles to the north of that village is a reminder of the source of eastern Mendip's wealth. In Norton St Philip we are back with the heritage of the wool trade as it flourished in the fifteenth and sixteenth centuries. This village is now inhabited mainly by Bath commuters, and agriculture is kept to the periphery. Until recently cows were driven through its streets, but the traffic now makes that impossible.

Yet it is still almost as good a village to wander in as Pepys found it to be, when he brought his wife to dine at the George on June 12th 1668, and pleased her with a commendation of her native county. He visited the church and made a diary note on the Fair Maids of Norton St Philip, a pair of Siamese twins "that had two bodies upward and one stomach and there lie buried". He did not mention the effigy of a fifteenth-century barrister, probably Sir John Fortescue, who became Lord Chief Justice of England. There he lies, complete with his high fur hat and his inkhorn, a portent of the future of a village whose inhabitants now mainly get their livelihood in offices.

Norton St Philip lies to the south of the Foss Way (as the Ordnance Survey spells it), which runs as the A367 south-west through Norton Radstock, which links Radstock to Midsomer Norton, and on past Downside Abbey to Oakhill and Shepton Mallet. Going more directly west, the turnpiked road to Wells goes past Chilcompton and over Old Down to Emborough.

In 1784, when he was eighteen, Richard Paget of East Cranmore compiled the history of Chilcompton as a contribution to Collinson's history of Somerset. He noted how the church stood alone, the houses around it having been removed more than a hundred years earlier when the Manor was enlarged. Ten years after Paget wrote his account, Coleridge came to Chilcompton, which he called Kirkhampton because of the dominance of its church. It was not that unrestored building that entranced him though, his pleasure was in the spring that fed the mill stream. Its waters tumbled over little waterfalls in the main street, where children

> With infant uproar and soul-soothing pranks,
> Releas'd from school, their little hearts at rest,
> Launch paper navies on thy waveless breast.

Emborough is also a place of water, although the serious anglers on the shores of the lake would not have much patience with toy boats let alone "soul-soothing pranks". Like Chilcompton, the village across the road to the west of the lake has almost entirely disappeared, but unlike it, little new housing has come to take its place. What remains is good. The church is no longer used, and beside its overgrown churchyard stands one of Mendip's oldest houses, parts of it dating from the thirteenth century.

Emborough Manor was once the home of the Hippsleys, who took over the waters that formed the fishponds when the monasteries were dissolved. The family, who were once known as the kings of Mendip, were like the Horners in their ambition for a great mansion. In the eighteenth century they achieved it, building the imposing house of Ston Easton, which no single family could possibly manage now. It owes its continued existence to the fact that it has become one of the most elegant and expensive hotels in the south-west.

Going west into Wells from Emborough, on the road once protected by the hill fort of Maesbury, the traveller is more conscious of Sedgemoor and the distant Quantock Hills than of the immediate hills of Mendip. The wide lowlands to the west and south are interspersed with "islands", lumps of jurassic rock emerging from what was once a reedy swamp and is now an *Alice in Wonderland* chess board of criss-cross rhynes and droves. Here Glastonbury Tor dominates the scene. It is exciting in any weather, etched against threatening black clouds, or becoming a real island again when the white mists replace the drained waters.

CHAPTER X

The Pressures of Leisure

MY NINE-YEAR-OLD grandson who lives in Canterbury, where there is not much opportunity for the sport, wanted to go caving. Once he had accepted that such an adventure could not be undertaken until he was a few years older, and that in any case it was not to be undertaken without considerable preparation and with experienced companions, he settled for Thomas Hardy's *Our Exploits at West Poley* as a bedtime story, and a walk, with torches, to the entrance of Goatchurch Cavern. Hardy's Mendip story is a marvellous tale for children, and should be required reading for quarrymen, for it treats of the disasters that can occur to a community if the flow of the underground water is disturbed.

The day we first went together to Goatchurch was an equal success. It was made so by the happy chance that once we had climbed the slippery, narrow path from Burrington Combe to Blackdown, and scrambled up to the cave's entrance among the undergrowth on the steep hillside, we found another small family party was there before us. Father was an experienced caver, who came regularly to Mendip from Buckinghamshire to explore the inside of these hills. His son, although a little older than Nicholas, was still really under age for these excursions. Yet their presence, and their lamps, allowed us to venture a little further into the rock than I would have otherwise allowed.

That tiny adventure, good enough at the time for us, does not begin to touch the real excitement and challenge that the Mendip limestone caves present to hundreds of people every year. There are many reasons for caving. They include the universal fascination of exploration, the exhilaration of difficult and hazardous physical exercise, the delight in unusual and seldom-seen aspects of nature, and an extension of our understanding of the beginnings of human life. Indeed, much of our knowledge of the early inhabitants of Mendip comes from the cavers who have deliberately explored the rock shelters in which both men and wild beasts once made their homes, as well as the chance findings of the quarrymen and miners who have kept alert to the history hidden in the limestone rocks.

Many of the caves were opened by chance. Lamb Leer Cavern at West Harptree, famed among cavers for the vast beehive-shaped stalagmite boss in its main chamber, was first discovered by miners in 1674, and then thoroughly explored by the mine owner, John Beaumont. The cave was abandoned in 1700, but reports of its existence persisted for nearly two hundred years when a reward was offered for its rediscovery.

In 1710 miners found bones, later recognized as the skeleton of an elephant, in Sandford caves; and in 1757 ochre miners came across a passage cave on the east side of Loxton Hill. That cave was lost in 1807, but not before Dr Catcott of Bristol had given an account of it in *The Gentleman's Magazine* and described the petrifications in the chambers, and the different colours which the iron and copper produced on the stone.

Many more discoveries were made during the nineteenth century. In 1825 miners at Banwell came across a cave almost completely filled with late Pleistocene bones. More bones were discovered the following year, when quarrymen working on the cliff beneath St Nicholas hilltop church at Uphill discovered the bones of elephant, rhinoceros, ox, horse, bear, hog and hyena as well as a coin of the Emperor Julian. In 1837, when the road going through Cheddar Gorge was widened, the cave which was immediately commercialized as a show place by Mr Cox was discovered.

Even now a few fresh caves are being opened up by members of the leading caving clubs (there are over 70 of them in Southern England) who spend their free time under Mendip. On an average some six hundred people enter the Mendip caves every week of the year, and at least twelve hostels have been set up for them in the hills. The clubs that are actually based on Mendip itself, and they include one at Sidcot school, have many advantages. The major discovery made by the Sidcot club was the intricate and difficult cave system approached through Longwood swallet, in the narrow valley above Cheddar Gorge. A swallet is the place where the water having emerged from the hill at a rising re-enters the limestone. So as its name suggests, the greatest hazard in the Longwood system, as in many other Mendip caves, is flash flooding.

One of the many odd differences between west and east Mendip lies in its caving terminology. The fairly elegant "swallet" of the west becomes the more forthright "slocker" of the east; but whatever name it goes under, it is flooding that has caused most cave disasters. Apart from that risk, cavers are naturally as prone to serious falls as any other people who climb about on rocks, and it is mainly those sort of accidents that the Mendip Rescue Organization has to cope with. It is a voluntary service, co-ordinated by Jim Hanwell, who has lived on Mendip all his life and who teaches geography at the Wells Blue School. He is adamant that caving should only take place in a responsible manner and with a majority of experienced people in each party. A large and reassuring person, who must transmit confidence to anybody in trouble, he was in charge of the rescue operation in November 1982, when to everyone's relief eleven cavers who had been trapped for thirteen hours emerged into the daylight.

Fortunately cave fatalities are astoundingly rare, considering the numbers of people who go in for the sport. The first recorded disaster was at Burrington Combe in 1874, in the cave known as Plumley's Hole. It is named after Joseph Plumley, an old quarryman, who lived alone in a nearby cottage with only a sheepdog for company. He offered to be lowered into the cave to investigate it, and after the initial success of that venture, tragedy struck. His neck was broken as he was being hauled to the surface to rejoin his dog.

Herbert Balch was one of the leading pioneers of serious caving on Mendip. He was fourteen when he first went underground, but it was several years after that before he entered his first large cave. That expedition was made with Thomas Willcox, then manager of the Priddy leadworks, and the cave that gave Balch his true initiation into the underworld of Mendip was probably Lamb Leer where he was to have his only major accident. It happened around the turn of the century, when a rope which had not been properly tested snapped as he was being lowered into the cave.

A generation of boys learnt the art and skill of caving from him, among them William Stanton, a Sidcot caver, who is now one of the foremost authorities on the underground systems of Mendip. He remembers that Balch was always meticulous in his approaches to safety precautions connected with his favourite sport, and that he took great care to preserve the nature of the territory he was exploring. In Stanton's own work in the caves, those considerations predominate.

Herbert Balch's precautions in no way dampened his enthusiasms. In the summer he would go caving immediately after work had finished at the Post Office and he had had his tea, often only returning to Wells in time to take up his official duties the next morning. At one time he rode out to the caves on a penny farthing bicycle, at others he went by train to Sandford and Banwell and then walked two and half miles to the caves. In 1904 he acquired a light governess cart, drawn by two successive donkeys, first Jack and then Jinnie. That way he travelled in some style to the scenes of his adventures, usually accompanied by his great black retriever, Rex, who actually went down Wookey Hole with him when he did his major excavations there.

In 1906 Balch became a founder member of the Mendip Nature Research Committee, an organization which made caving central to the exploration of the natural history of the hills. Indeed, his own work on all aspects of the natural and human history of the area has proved to be a source of enthusiasm which is still running today. Mr Young of Shipham, who was lucky enough to help Balch with some excavations at Rookham in the hills above Wells, is one of the many people who have owed a lifetime's interest in Mendip's history to that mentor. Balch was interested in all aspects of the past from the Bronze Age barrow builders to the remains of the nineteenth-century lead mining.

The excavations that Balch and his friends were engaged in, and the discoveries in the Mendip caves in the early years of this century, did not just reveal that there were settlements on Mendip many thousands of years ago; they also tell us a little of what life was like for the people who lived here then. Read's cavern, which lies below a ledge of rock on the lower slopes of Backdown to the east of Rowberrow wood, disclosed an Iron Age tragedy after it had been opened up in 1919 by the University of Bristol Speleological Society. Ten years of excavation revealed that several of the Celtic inhabitants of the cave had been killed when a major fall of rock blocked their entrance. Among the objects that were found beside their bones was an iron horse hobble designed with much more care and elegance than its function required, its elaborately curved links resembling the Celtic designs of a much later period. With it were some pottery, and two bronze brooches dating from around the middle of the second century BC.

It was fortunate that Read's cavern was discovered fairly late, when its finds could be handled by specialists in prehistory. The barrows of Mendip, like those on the limestone of Derbyshire's White Peak, suffered from the fashionable antiquarian enthusiasms of eighteenth-century landowners and leisured clergy, who opened them almost at random and made little consistent attempts to record their finds systematically. With the nineteenth century came a somewhat more careful and responsible attitude to the past. Men like the unhappy Skinner may have found time spent digging into prehistory a welcome escape from their present miseries, but they took care to see that their excavations were carried out as carefully as the knowledge of their times allowed.

Now that archaeology has become a science, and archaeological sites are protected by government departments, the Mendip barrows are saved from any further ruthless handling. Much of what has been found in them in the past can now be seen in the big national museums and in the cases of local history societies. Arranging these fragments of the past, caring for them, and generally trying to find out a bit more about them is probably more fun than looking at them. Visitors to the collections, caught by rain or boredom, usually scurry past the prehistory to the agricultural, industrial and domestic displays that can start them off on reminiscences of their own or their parents' past. The more distant centuries cannot be brought indoors; it takes the high mound of an undug long barrow, like that on the steep ridge to the north of Chewton Mendip, to make time jump that far.

Industrial archaeology is a different matter. The lead mining collection at Wells museum deals with an understandable human activity, and although the processes of the work may not be fully understood they can be discussed. Yet still things are even better in the field. The Mendip Society found plenty of enthusiasts who were willing to brave cold weather in order to help with the restoration of the lead flues at Charterhouse, and to clear the land round Fussell's iron works at Mells.

Mendip is fortunate in the people who give up their time to recording its past. Among them are professional historians like Frances Neale of Winscombe and Michael McGarvie of Frome, who have the ability and imagination to bring life out of ancient charters and legal documents. Others, with no professional qualifications in history, have devoted most of their spare time to recording the way people have lived in these hills. It is an exploration that will never completely be done, but the charts on which successive generations of local historians may draw have been mainly compiled by Robin Atthill, a former teacher of English at Downside, who has lived on Mendip nearly all his life. His childhood was spent at Compton Martin in the north-west, and his most active retirement is based in a cottage on the outskirts of Oakhill. So he straddles both east and west of this divided area, and has seen the whole region through many changes. As a young boy he could look out over the farmlands which now lie under Chew Valley lake; and when his parents moved to Ebbor Hall, he knew the narrow roads of Cheddar before they became choked with tourists and the traders that prey on them.

Inspired by Robin Atthill's love of his native hills, the Downside boys started an Industrial Archaeology group, investigating most of the sites in the area under the direction of their teacher and colleague, and making extensive drawings of them. In these out-of-school local studies, they were carrying on the tradition of Father Ethelbert Horne, a monk at Downside and parish priest of Stratton-on-the-Fosse, who celebrated his love of Mendip by devoting his rare spare hours to compiling several volumes of stories and essays on its past. Now the Downside tradition of local studies is in the hands of the present headmaster, Father Philip Jebb, who finds Mendip "the most wonderful part of the world to live in". A grandson of Hilaire Belloc, that much loved popularizer of antiquarian studies, he runs the school archaeological club as well as having a public involvement with the Somerset Record Society.

Father Philip's grandfather knew the delight of tracing old roads, and that is a pleasure that is shared by an increasing number of people, walking through fields on rights of way that were established long before enclosures, or stepping out along the footpaths which have been connected to form the West Mendip Way, a long-distance path which starts by the playing fields of the Blue School in Wells and goes east to Bleadon. Walking is the most gentle of pleasures, yet even walking can strain and alter the character of a place as more and more people join in with ramblers' clubs, take part in sponsored walks and runs, and spend days on field trips arranged in conjunction with adult classes in local and natural history.

For the people of Bath and Bristol, the Mendip hills are the natural place for a day out, and any fine weekend will bring them in hundreds to Crook Peak, Blackdown and Velvet Bottom. From farther afield coach loads of holiday makers come to the more obvious tourist attractions of the area: Wells, Cheddar Gorge, Burrington Combe and Wookey Hole. All over the world tourism makes money for the places it destroys, and that is how things are in Cheddar Gorge. When the caves were opened up at the beginning of this century at an entry fee of a shilling, and visitors aproached them from the village in horse-drawn charabancs, no one could foretell the thousands of people who would be making their way to them each day at the height of the season, and paying almost £2 to enter the limestone.

Cheddar's answer to Herbert Balch of Wells was Richard Cox Gough, a nephew of the Cox who opened a cave in the Gorge in 1837. A former sea captain from Bristol, Gough fell on hard times and came to Cheddar in the 1880s, where he lived in the Gorge and got work in the Priddy mines at two shillings a day. With ten children to support and a miner's instinct for exploiting the underworld of the hills, he was soon adding to his income by taking parties of the gentry into a cave on the top of Cheddar Gorge.

The success of that venture made him look nearer home, where an old couple actually lived in a cave in the side of the Gorge, its entrance barred with a stout wooden door. Gough, realizing the potential of their rocky home, built Jack and Nancy a cottage in exchange for it, and the deal was even more fortunate than he had expected. When he explored and blasted his way over the stalagmites into the depths of the cave, he found a great chamber. So intense was his delight, that, being a very religious man, he immediately sent for all his family to scramble in after him, and had them falling on their knees, to sing hymns among the towering rock formations. Intensely romantic as well as religious, Gough was not just thinking of the profits to come when he made that gesture. In any case, singing sounds very good in a cave, as the Banwell choir appreciated about half a century earlier. The Reverend William Phelps reported that after the bone cave had been discovered, "the village choir conceiving this vaulted apartment would give a fine effect to their voices, descended into it, and exercised their vocal powers much to their own satisfaction".

The grandeur of the caves inspired their own hymns. The Reverend E. B. Burrows, writing in 1849, had just about light enough to see the beautiful colours of the rock formations:

> Here deep within the bowels of the land
> Shrouded in night, the caverned wonders stand.
> And vaulted arch and marble galleries rise,
> Clothed in a vest of amber draperies.

Gough wrote his own Mendip meditation to the glory of God. It contained the verses:

My God, who raised the Mendip range,
 Out of the ocean bed;
And split and rent these hills that tower
 So high above my head.

In seeming darkness He has worked
 In caves unseen by man,
Great wonders He has brought to light:
 In wisdom laid the plan.

In the hills to the east of Cheddar, where the Axe emerges from the rock, Wookey Hole, now the most extensive and magnificent of the show caves, was "brought to light" in Gough's sense thousands of years ago. But it was in 1927, when the electric light was first installed, that the general public had access to it. That light has altered its character a little. Now luxuriant ferns flourish on its wet rocks.

In 1929, Herbert Balch published a book entirely devoted to the wonders of Wookey Hole, dedicating his work to the cave's owners, Captain and Mrs G. W. Hodgkinson "whose bold enterprise in opening up this Great Cave is giving pleasure to many people".

Before that time the cave was an elitist pleasure. The few visitors who entered the cavern took candles with them, and in later years if they were lucky enough to have a guide, he might throw a flare of benzoline on to the surface of the Axe. The Reverend C. F. Metcalfe saw that, and celebrated the experience for posterity:

A glow, a gleam, a broader beam,
Startle those realms of ancient Night;
While bats whirl round on slanting wing,
Astonished at this awful thing.
The rock roof's reflected rays
Are caught up in the waterways,
And every jewelled stalactite
Is bathed in that stupendous light.

Even with the pressure of today's crowds the grandeur of this cave holds its own; with its great domed roof in the main chamber, whose size no human architect could ever achieve, and the underground Axe flowing silently along the cave floor. People have lived here ever since Mendip was settled, and they went on doing so intermittently until the seventeenth century, by which time visitors from all over England were including what Michael Drayton called "Ochy's dreadful hole" in their West Country tours.

Celia Fiennes came here in 1698, and like many another visitor she was impressed with the way that water works on the stone in underground passages to form sculptured shapes, and she tried her hand at explaining the process. She perceived that the underground Axe "looks cleer to the bottom which is all full of stones as is the sides, just like candy or like the branches they put in the boyling of copperace for the copperice to crust about it, this in the same manner so that the water congeales here into stone and does as it were bud or grow out one stone out of another; where ever this water drops it does not weare the rock in hollow as some other subterranian caves does, but it hardens and does increase the stone and that in a roundness as if it candy's as it fell, which I am of opinion it does, so it makes the rocks grow and meet each other in some places".

Like everyone else she was struck by the way the rocks so formed resembled people, animals and objects. She noted the names the local people gave them, including, of course, the famous witch who was believed to have made the cave for her enchantment. Certainly Celia was enchanted by it. "The rocks are glistening and shine like diamonds," she wrote in her journal, "and some you climbe over where one meetes with the congealed drops of water just like icicles hanging down; some of the stones is white like alabaster and glisters like mettle." At least Celia was content to record her delight in words, and one likes to think that even had she been given the opportunity, she would not have behaved in the disgraceful fashion of the poet, Alexander Pope, who committed the disgusting sacrilege of having the Wookey Hole stalactites shot down so that he could set them up in his grotto in Twickenham.

A few years later, literary London was again indirectly affected by the Mendip hills, when Dr Fox of Brislington realized that the seaside village of Weston, just to the north of Bleadon, was suitable for a health resort. It was the iodine in the ozone which rises from the mud at low tide which was supposed to be so good for you, and the tide here goes out a very long way indeed. Dr Johnson's friend Mrs Piozzi appreciated it. She wrote to Sir James Fellowes of Bognor Regis, declaring that although the little place "was neither gay nor fashionable . . . the Breezes here are most salubrious — no land nearer than North America". These salubrious breezes were potent enough for the benevolent to feel that they should be widely shared, and in 1820 a sea-bathing infirmary designed "for the purpose of extending sea-bathing to the poor, who suffer from scrofulous diseases" was set up at nearby Uphill.

John Rutter, who published his account of north-west Somerset in 1829, was not so impressed by the large tracts of beach left by the ebb of the spring tide. The Weston of his time had 250 houses and a hotel, but it was already starting to grow rapidly. Like Mrs Piozzi, he found the place deficient in fashionable amusements although it was serving as a "constant resort of genteel visitors". However he did have a few good words to say for the bathing machines, finding them "well built, and kept clean and tidy. They are constantly in attendance except at very low tides, and may be driven to any requisite depth with the tide". They were not much consolation to poor John Skinner, who brought his family to Weston for a short holiday from Camerton in the July of 1832. They all agreed it was "a wretched place to continue in for any length of time".

Nevertheless others thought differently and from 1850 to 1900 the population of Weston rose from four to eighteen thousand, helped partly by the railway, which had reached the town in 1841. At that time it was not felt to be a welcome addition to a place just beginning to take advantage of the British discovery of the seaside holiday. So the line had to be diverted to the moor to the east of the town, where the station was set up. The trains were then drawn into Weston by horses along a short branch line.

Weston did not become any more fashionable or gay during this century, but before continental holidays became widespread, it provided countless families with good sea air, wide sandy beaches and a chance to walk in Woodspring woods and on the uplands of Brean Down and Sand Point.

The seaboard of Mendip stretches from Weston through Uphill and Brean to Burnham-on-Sea and, like any other stretch of seaside, it has become a popular retirement area. That is true of Mendip as a whole, and has been so since the eighteenth century when some of the most elegant houses on the hills were built. Now the pattern is for dreadful mock stone bungalows, which wreck the view their occupants have come to enjoy. This desecration of the landscape is somewhat counterbalanced by the numbers of ruined or dilapidated ancient cottages and farmhouses that have been pleasantly restored by leisured people.

Apart from some lapses into architectural bad taste, the people who choose Mendip for their retirement make a welcome contribution of time and specialized interests to the area, running local preservation and amenity societies, and adding to the general understanding of the natural and human history of the hills. In return Mendip can give them both nature and art. It is true that the nearest theatres of any repute are now in Bristol and Bath, although that was not always so. Wells had a theatre in the eighteenth century, demolished to make room for new housing; but, like many another small provincial town, the city was able to boast a repertory company in the inter-war years.

Music in Wells has not diminished. The Cathedral School draws leading musicians from all over the country, and their performances inspire the local choirs and orchestras to achieve near-professional standards. There is a long tradition here of music-making by church groups and private *ensembles*, which has culminated in the performances given by the Bevan family of Croscombe.

Claver Morris, a doctor in Wells from 1684 to 1726, would have been at home with the Bevans; and they might have enjoyed going with him on September 22nd 1709, when he took a group of friends to Shepton Mallet church to try out the new organ. Every Tuesday he climbed the stone steps that lead out of the south end of Vicars Close to attend music meetings in the medieval hall. He was one of the main organizers of a monthly carnival meeting called the Moon Feast because it was always held on the night of the full moon so that country members could get into the city. Driving over Mendip in the dark can still present some problems. Later The Mutual Entertainment was felt to be a more suitable title for the gatherings, and it is one that could describe the meetings of most Mendip societies today, and that in no way detracts from the serious purpose of their aims.

CHAPTER XI

The Inheritors

"Conservation has to be learned and taught, it's not part of human nature to say 'I like this place therefore I will leave it for others to enjoy'." Dr W. I. Stanton. *Transactions of the British Cave Research Association* September 1982.

DR CLAVER MORRIS was a man who liked the place he lived in and who also liked societies. Today's Mendip Society would surely have liked him, despite the astonishment he would certainly have shown could he have seen its members spending a cold, wet Easter Sunday afternoon looking around Priddy mineries. In any case the place would be unrecognizable to him, for the visible remains of the flues and mine buildings all date from the nineteenth-century re-smelting, and Forestry Commission conifers struggle to grow in the leaded gruffy ground of Stock Hill. Yet Priddy nine barrows on the skyline to the north would reassure him; and despite our jeans and anoraks and gentry voices, he would find our absorption in the industrial and natural history of these high acres understandable enough.

"What do you make of it all?" he might have asked us as we scrambled in and out of the gruffs. Yet when that question was put to us, it did not come from any seventeenth-century ghost, but from a London member of a caving club, who had bought the land some twenty years ago, and who now spends much of his spare time trying to get trees to grow in its lead-filled soil. This does not prevent the public walking across it, and the area surrounding the old St Cuthbert mine, together with the deep (some say bottomless) pools that supplied the water for washing the ore, is managed by the Somerset Trust for Nature Conservation. It is a place of lizards, grass snakes, slow-worms and adders. Its waters attract crested newts and dragon-flies, and here you can find emperor moths and several unusual plants.

The Somerset Trust has professional biologists as its officials, but its members are mostly amateur naturalists. Its function is to preserve areas of particular ecological importance, and in Dr Stanton's terms to teach conservation. As in the case of Priddy, this Trust does not always own the land it manages. On the other hand, the Kenneth Allsop Trust, set up in memory of a beloved naturalist and broadcaster, is both owner and manager of Steep Holm island, an isolated lump of oolitic limestone, 950 yards long and 350 wide, emerging out of the turbulent waters of the Bristol Channel, five miles off shore from Weston-super-Mare.

The Kenneth Allsop Trust bought this island (the Holmness of Quiller Couch's *True Tilda*) in 1976. They cleared it of the ravages of waves of invading vandals, and started to transform a piece of land which has been used as hermitage, military base and smallholding into a nature reserve. It is a unique habitat. For the novelist, John Fowles, it appears to have "wandered in from another, more tropical latitude — an impression some of its characteristic flower species do not contradict when one actually lands".

The landing is still quite an adventure, even though a boat load of tourists is admitted to the island every Wednesday and Saturday throughout the summer, for the currents round the island are the fastest in any English waters. No one can expect to make the five-mile journey without a wetting, and there is always a possibility of having to stay overnight on the island if the weather turns.

As soon as the visitor climbs the rocky path which leads to the top of the island, he is confronted by the most prolific of Steep Holm's flora — the alexanders, a wild carrot, which was grown in the Middle Ages as a pot herb, and which I am told tastes like celery. More rare are the wild leek, and the famous Mediterranean pink peony, which blooms here in May and June. The monks who introduced it to the island in the Middle Ages used its roots as a specific against epilepsy.

Unlike the rest of western Mendip, which is a natural habitat for adders, the only reptiles on Steep Holm are the bluish slow-worms. The main natural interest of the island is provided by its birds. Cormorants nest and fish from its north bank, and there is a hope that the peregrine falcons, who were last seen here in 1954, may be returning. But it is above all a gull colony, and in the nesting season it is almost a challenge to walk across the island, the parent birds are so defensive of the vulnerable eggs in the crowded nests which huddle together on the rocky ledges. Yet a greater hazard than the feet of careless walkers threatens the birds. These scavengers on man's waste are constantly dying from the shred of plastic which they pick up among the food thrown out in the dustbins of Weston-super-Mare. The Kenneth Allsop Trust is powerless to intervene in that disaster.

Several more bureaucratically official bodies are involved in the tasks of conserving and monitoring other areas of Mendip. The University of Bristol has 80 acres around Ubley Warren Farm adjoining the Blackmoor Educational nature reserve at Charterhouse, but it is the Nature Conservancy Council which is responsible for managing most Mendip sites. That work depends on the co-operation of the local farmers, for grazing is essential if the balance of vegetation is to be maintained. Hawthorn, gorse and bracken quickly take over land that is not put to any other use, and choke the other plants that might flourish there.

One of the most visited areas to be managed by the Nature Conservancy Council (in this instance on behalf of the National Trust) is Ebbor Gorge: 116 acres of woodland presented to the nation in memory of Sir Winston Churchill in 1972 by Mrs G. W. Hodgkinson of Wookey Hole. Tom Hodgson is employed by the Council to look after this spectacular rift in the hills, whose heights offer a majestic view across the Somerset levels and Polden ridge to the Quantocks. He came here from a nature conservancy on the Pennines, and has exchanged his remote home, four miles from the nearest neighbour, for a terrace house in Wells. It is a reminder that his present task is one of preserving wildlife in the face of constant human pressure. For the past six years Mr Hodgson has worked with teams of volunteers, some of whom come from local schools, to ensure that the thousands of visitors to Ebbor Gorge each year are able to appreciate it properly without doing too much harm to its individual character.

There are rare birds of prey here, a few red deer, and a wealth of lichens and unusual plants which all need protecting. Above all it is essential that the delicate screes on either side of the narrow path leading up to the gorge should be watched whenever people are about, for the stones could easily be dislodged by unthinking scramblers. If they went, colonies of plants, insects and small mammals would be disturbed, and the gorge would be irretrievably changed. For that reason no one is supposed to visit this reserve between dusk and daybreak.

Yet, Mr Hodgson, who believes that "most of Mendip is really a site of Special Scientific Interest", still welcomes the visitors whose inroads make the land he manages so vulnerable. Carefully made steps through the anemone-filled woods lead the walker down to the valley bottom; and above them, by the car park, a special nature trail has been designed for the disabled. That is not the only service that Ebbor has given to the rest of the community, for when three hundred diseased elms had to be felled, pupils from Wells Cathedral School distributed the wood to the elderly and disabled. The gap those sick trees left has been more than filled by plantings of the oaks, alders and willows which are native to Mendip.

Apart from Ebbor Gorge, the National Trust has three other Mendip properties: Brean Down; the north of Cheddar Gorge, which is thus saved from the vulgar rash of tourist attractions on its lower slopes; and Tor Hill at Wells. Plants as well as landscapes are preserved in all these places, although there was a local uproar when some ancient yews were cut down on Tor Hill so that the land available to be let for grazing could be extended.

Few visitors to Wells would think of walking in Tor woods at the north-eastern edge of the city; but in the Cheddar woods the pressures are enormous. Over two million people visit the Gorge each year, and although they do not all walk in the woods, enough people make their way there to present a serious threat to the quality of the landscape and its wildlife. Bill Butcher, formerly of the Somerset Trust, which manages most of the area, exercised his responsibility for the three reserves at the top of the Gorge by drawing up nature trails for the visitors, and arranging evening and Sunday walks in the summer to which holiday makers were invited. People who know what they are looking for are much less likely to damage a place.

The three reserves are reached from Black Rock Drove to the west of the Gorge. That area was bought by the National Trust from the Amey Roadstone Corporation and so saved from death by quarrying. Black Rock itself is a rocky wooded hill opposite a small quarry which was worked before mechanical devices tore into the hills. Its modest ravages are softened and partly screened by hawthorn and wayfaring trees.

The drove runs between hill and quarry to the two other reserves: Longwood, which runs up to Lower Farm at Charterhouse; and Velvet Bottom, which winds its way between rocky banks and gruffy ground to Charterhouse. It is a placid, happy place, whose smooth short turf reflects its name. Its profusion of wild flowers would give the casual visitor no indication that its soil has been so blighted by lead that no trees have grown here for over a hundred years. That may not be a hopeless situation, however, for a new tree-planting programme has recently been initiated.

The 42 acres of Longwood, cared for and coppiced by Bill Butcher's volunteers, are a favourite haunt for both naturalists and cavers; and a pleasure enough for any walker whether or not he is following any specific interest.

That pleasure is fragile. The Somerset Trust's volunteer wardens do their best to protect it on the reserves, but all stretches of the countryside that are open to the public are subject to abuse. Motor cyclists are being successfully kept away from the paths through the Priddy and Charterhouse mineries, but they still roar along the green lane of the Fosse Way up to Beacon Hill, and scramble through the East Harptree woods around the earthworks of Richmont Castle, despite the responsible attitude of most motor cycle clubs in steering their members away from vulnerable ground.

It is no new thing for visitors, and most of the motor cyclists come from surrounding towns, to irritate the natives. In 1877 the Reverend W. Jackson complained in his *Visitors' Handbook to Weston-super-Mare* that "the patience of Weston constables gets sorely taxed by the less educated arrivals from Bristol, Newport and Cardiff. It must be added in fairness that the amount of material damage done at these times is smaller than might have been reasonably apprehended; though the visitations themselves promote neither the morality nor yet the prosperity of Weston".

Weston seems to have survived that onslaught, though no place is ever quite as prosperous as it would like to be, and probably not as moral either. Nor are those qualities the ones that are really seriously at risk from the crowds of tourists who come on to the heights of Mendip. It is impossible to subject a stretch of wild country to a summer influx of thousands of people, and expect its natural life to be undisturbed. Yet people do use the countryside more responsibly than they did some years ago. At least the picking of wild flowers and the collecting of birds' eggs are activities of the past. Although the rare Cheddar pink and Steep Holm's peonies have to be carefully guarded from the unenlightened enthusiast, everyone can enjoy the billows of pale-mauve cuckoo spit in spring; the white banks of ransoms in the summer woods; and the final flourish of smokey-blue cranesbill along the sides of the roads in August.

Less obvious, but more exciting to the naturalist, are the rare white rock rose by the western seaboard and the hawkweed, which is unique to this stretch of limestone. The mossy saxifrage, cut-leaved self-heal, autumn crocus and rare blue groomwell can all be found at the top of

Cheddar Gorge, which is also the only home of the delicate Cheddar pink, which flowers in June on the dizzy edges of the rock pinnacles. In the woods there are lily of the valley, Solomon's Seal and a dwarf member of the teazle family. Ebbor Gorge is rich with the greater butterfly orchid, the nettle-leaved bell flower and the bloody cranesbill. Sea campion grows on the old lead workings at Priddy and Charterhouse, together with the sea storkbill. Both these hardy plants can flourish in lead-infested soil. They also serve as a reminder of the period when the sea covered the Somerset levels and the southern slopes of Mendip were coastal cliffs.

Plants often flourish in areas where men have seriously disrupted the landscape, as anyone who has given much attention to motorway verges will have noticed. Railway cuttings have always provided a rich habitat for wild flowers, and in 1869 Frank Knight was recording that the banks beside the new track had attracted a profusion of moth mullian. Now sleepers and rails have gone, and in most parts their place has been taken with such a profusion of brambles and grasses that the more colourful plants have been choked out of existence. Yet Mendip is still, as it has always been, an area rich in a variety of plants.

It was a Dean of Wells, Dr William Turner, who is generally considered to be the father of English botany. He produced his *Herball* in the middle of the sixteenth century, and wrote of a particular kind of barley which he had not seen in this country "saving at Welles in my garden"; and of the wild flax which he found within a mile of Wells, "it hath fewer boles in the top than the sown flax hath, and a great deal longer stalk". Dr Turner's mantle as Mendip botanist fell on the stalwart shoulders of Ella Goold, a Wells woman and former teacher, who died during a rambling and botanizing holiday in the Himalayas in the late summer of 1983. From Herbert Balch's daughter, Margaret, she inherited the task of keeping the city museum constantly supplied, week by week, with specimens of the wild flowers currently in bloom in the area.

As for animals, Mendip hares are sandy, black-pointed creatures, much rarer than their reddish East Anglian counterparts; but I have seen three of them in the course of a short February walk. But of all mammals it is the badgers, accused of carrying bovine TB, which are the most talked-about animal on Mendip. It is quite usual to come across their sets in the woods, but the only badger I have seen here was a dead one, killed by a car and put up beside the main road on a gate post in Temple Cloud. Such a carcass would not have been seen in that manner in the early years of this century, when badgers were classified as vermin, and a shilling could be earned by presenting a dead one to the authorities. Foxes were also rated at a shilling, rats fetched fourpence, hedgehogs and polecats twopence each, mice were a penny a dozen, the same price as sparrows, although a dozen bullfinches (still known by the local name of "whoops") made a shilling.

In 1912, while that tariff was still current, the bird sanctuary on Brean Down was set up, with ravens among the inmates. Ravens nested on Cheddar cliffs then, and together with peregrines they could be found on Callow Hill, but the red-legged chough which once bred on Mendip had already disappeared. Now the best places for bird watching are the reservoirs of Axbridge, Blagdon and Chew Valley, whose waters attract great numbers and varieties of birds.

The management of woodlands as well as water can make drastic changes to the natural habitat. Since the middle of the fourth millennium BC, when its oaks were used to build the trackways that have been discovered under the peat of the Somerset levels, Mendip woodland has been exploited and diminished. Ash, oak and lime are the native trees, solid broad leaf which permit a rich ground flora. Billingsley, pontificating about woodlands, as he did about all other aspects of land management, claimed that they were "not only an ornament to the respective seats to which they belong, but are in themselves a fertile source of annual profit". It is interesting to speculate as to how he would have reacted to the sources of annual profit represented by the conifers which now cover such large areas of the hills.

In addition to the private woodlands, the Forestry Commission extends over 2300 acres. The head forester is Mr R. A. Liddell, who came to the area in 1978, inheriting a crop that was mostly planted during the war years, and which was planned on a 55-year rotation. He has a broad-leaf planting programme in hand, motivated partly by considerations of amenity, but also by the increased value of hard wood for domestic fuel. If his plans come to fruition Rowberrow should emerge with a 120-acre beech wood, and beech woods together with mixed woodlands will spread across Beacon Hill to East and West Cranmore. Meanwhile Mr Liddell is conscious that Mendip is a place for recreation, so the public are welcome to walk and ride through much of the forest; orienteers can practise their demanding sport along identical paths flanked by close-growing trees, which shut out all hope of steering a course by the sun; while naturalists are able to use forest habitats for studying such specialist topics as moths and fungi.

The reservoirs have altered the face of Mendip more permanently and as markedly as the conifers. Four hundred and fifty acres of farmland went to make Blagdon Lake in 1901; and in 1938 a bill was brought before Parliament to sanction Bristol Waterworks' purchase of two thousand acres of Chew Valley, with the intention of flooding fourteen hundred of them. The project was eventually put into force after the war. The hamlet of Moreton, the remains of a gunpowder mill and the site of a Roman villa were drowned, but the greatest loss was the agricultural land, which the National Farmers Union vainly tried to preserve by wholeheartedly opposing the flooding.

In any case, farmers know only too well that water is a perpetual problem in areas of porous limestone, and after even a moderate storm the water pours out of the hills, a red turbulence floods the lanes, making farm gates impassable, swirling sticks and mud into the streets of towns, and forcing farmers to keep the cattle in stalls late into the spring lest the fields get churned up beyond redemption. Matters are often made worse because the old river channels and mill races, which used to be kept clear, have silted up, and in some stretches they have been deliberately narrowed.

At the same time, those industries which do continue to use the rivers have frequently been guilty of polluting the water supply. That is a danger that most people including the industrialists are now constantly aware of. "The mill is here because of the river," says Mr Peter McLean of Inveresk Paper Mill at Wookey, "and we are going to protect it." Pollution of the water can come about through much more apparently insignificant causes than the effluent of large industrial undertakings. In the eighteenth century there were complaints against the keeping of ducks in Mells, for they were "an annoyance to the waters". More seriously, John Smith of Leigh was taken to task for "washing Bellies and Insides of Cattel in the water course" and "so fouling the same to the prejudice and annoyance of the inhabitants". Agriculture still presents a hazard to the water supply, especially now that pesticides and chemical fertilizers are added to the slurry; even sheep dip can pollute the waters by taking toxic waters down the swallets. Mells river is still at risk as it flows from Gurney Slade to Frome. It joins the river Frome about half a mile downstream from the town, where it receives a discharge of municipal and industrial waste.

If one of the proposed schemes for erecting a Severn Barrage between England and Wales should ever be put into effect, the course of Mendip waters, now relatively controlled, would be profoundly disturbed; and the effective and historic drainage of the levels rendered useless. The purpose of the whole undertaking would be to harness the river's tidal flow in order to produce hydrotidal energy. In many ways the scheme, which was first contemplated as long ago as 1923, is attractive, for the fourteen- to fifteen-metre tide range is only exceeded by the sixteen metres at Ungara Bay, Canada. However, its construction would involve building a fifteen-mile dam across the channel from Brean Down to the Welsh coast, and there is a distinct possibility that the whole of Steep Holm would be quarried away for its construction.

It is all still speculation. The scheme that is currently on the drawing board leaves both the Holms intact, and envisages the barrage going to the west of them. However it is achieved, a Severn barrage would make a greater difference to the Severn Sea than was effected by the transformation of the Zuider Zee into the IJsselmeer. The plan is that the turbulent shallow waters to the east of the barrage would become a vast pleasure lake and yacht marina; although a few unpleasantly realistic voices do enquire as to what would become of the sewage from the surrounding conurbations which is presently pumped into these waters. That is a matter that will become more urgent if ever sufficient money to build the barrage should be found; and it would probably only be economically possible if enough industry moved into the area for the proposed conurbation of Severnside, running right round the estuary as Southend is linked to Chatham, to become a reality.

Meanwhile the fiercest opposition to the scheme comes from the people of Burnham-on-Sea, and those who live at the edge of the levels beneath the southern scarp of Mendip. They have reason to fear. If the whole of the Ungara Bay scheme were ever to be put into operation there would be six inches of water over Boston airport at high tide and parts of the city would be flooded. The new housing estates by the Burnham sand dunes could expect a much worse fate.

Those who are against the scheme, but in favour of reducing the amount of energy supplied by nuclear power, argue that it would be much more satisfactory to put the money into a really effective programme of conservation and insulation, and in the second place that a series of small schemes around the country, which would provide a more even power supply, would be a much more acceptable alternative.

As things are, the two greatest threats to Mendip come from the use of agricultural land and buildings, and quarrying. In the country it is the landowners who hold the key to Mendip's conservation. If the cynical are right when they say that farmers would rather do anything with their fields than farm them, then the developers are bound to rush in and the hills be transformed into housing estates, caravan parks and gaping quarries. As it is, Sedgemoor and Mendip District Councils have to be constantly vigilant, or rashes of bungalows put up for permanent or holiday use would appear overnight. Local estate agents say that there is always more than sufficient demand for these, particularly in the favourite commuter area of the Chew valley. Yet the District Councils do make some very silly rulings which frustrate imaginative building and preservation. Any new building, however modest, has to have a surfaced access to it, even if the owner would be quite happy to approach his house along a field path; and planning permission is often refused for the conversion of old barns into dwellings if they are sited too far away from the normal services. The thought of people generating their own electricity, or managing without it, appals the municipal mind.

In the towns also the planners have both great successes and lamentable failures in the conservation of buildings. Mendip District Council protects much of Frome, including Keyford, where the old tannery was, as a conservation area. Yet it is left to private bodies, such as the Frome Historic Buildings Trust, which has recently bought several doomed houses on the once elegant Vallis Way, to look after their own areas at a considerable cost to public generosity. If the money had not been found, then it is more than likely that some private developer would have been empowered to bulldoze a whole terrace of character and history, and replace it with faceless but convenient modern dwellings. It happens everywhere, the whole character of a place is lost for ever, and this loss is not entirely the fault of population growth, extreme as that has been. For five hundred years, until 1951, the population of Wells was a steady five thousand. Now the city has to struggle to limit its numbers to ten thousand people. Many of them have to live in the plastic, instant houses in the ugly estates that surround the medieval city. While some may enjoy the convenience and comfort, others might well prefer one of the many stone cottages which are being allowed to fall into decay.

The balance between old and new is no easier to achieve in the case of farm buildings. Many beautiful barns and outhouses are allowed to fall into decay, while the work of the farm goes on in ugly factory sheds. No planning permission is needed for farm buildings, provided that not more than five thousand square feet of buildings are erected every two years. Farmhouses can suffer too. The Cloford farmer, who lives in a characterless but comfortable modern house while his beautiful manor farmhouse falls into decay and spends its last untended years as a store, has the right to choose comfort, but surely not at the price of such neglect.

The story is not all gloomy. Some farmers, such as Alfred Gay of East Harptree, are prepared to go to great lengths to preserve historic farm buildings; while other houses have been saved by people dedicated enough to restore them as dwellings though they do not necessarily want to farm the land. Their devotion cannot always save the farm buildings. Lower Farm is most beautifully restored now, but the massive stone Longhouse Barn, which Bill Young remembers from his years on the edge of Longwood, is a roofless ruin.

At Eastwood, Alfred Gay does at least get some help with his repairs from the Ministry of Works. But that would not go far with anyone less concerned than he and his three sons that the buildings should be kept up as far as possible in their original state. When that model farm steading was built, the Eastwood estate was owned by William Taylor, a former butler at Gurney Court, who married the daughter of the family. Her inheritance went into the farm buildings, which cost £1500. It would take over £6000 now just to repoint them. Cornish stone masons, who had worked on the reclamation of the old lead mines, were employed to do the building. They were paid a pittance for their labours, and the stone they worked with was quarried out of the farm land. The quarry ground was subsequently filled in, a piece of conservation natural to those times.

With the collapse of the North Somerset railway in which he had considerable financial interest, Taylor went bankrupt. The farm passed into the hands of Charles Adam Kemble, rector of Bath, who established his sons here. In 1915 Mr Gay's maternal grandfather, Alfred Lovell, moved in and took over 146 acres of the home farm. The family has been there ever since.

Despite their long connection with Eastwood, Mr Gay and his sons are unusual in their willingness to take so much time and trouble to convert the old to new uses. They have even supplied electric power to the old steam thresher, but on the whole we do have to be prepared to sacrifice some amenities to convenience. That is no new story, and it is all too easy to be romantic about the simple rural life while forgetting all the disadvantages. Gas works, for example, may be unsightly, but they were hymned at Sidcot in 1842:

> Hail to the Gas-works! hail the pleasing day
> When from they walls O Sidcot! far away
> Are banished and dismissed in hopeless tramp
> The greasy oil can and ill-scented lamp.

Nowadays it is the quarries that are at the centre of the conflict between the desire to preserve the landscape and the insatiable needs of a technological society. Quarries provide employment (although not nearly as much as the massive scale of the undertakings could lead you to believe) and they are an essential part of the road building system. It is easy to be romantic about the gruffy ground of the lead miners, and even complain when farmers level off their land by bulldozing out remains of rakes and buddle pits, for there is no fear that lead mining on Mendip will ever be revived. And it is easy to be angry about individual outrages like the removal of Mendip's thin topsoil at Green Ore for sale to garden centres. That is a sad reflection of the even greater outrage taking place a few miles away on the Somerset levels, where the irreplaceable peat is being removed wholesale for the same luxury market.

The quarries are a different matter. The nation needs limestone, and Mendip is glad to supply it, but there is a great difference between removing the stone from hills by manpower, even with the aid of a bit of gunpowder, and tearing the rock away with vast and sophisticated machines.

Mendip people started to be seriously conscious of the threat from the quarries during this century. Before the First World War Cheddar Gorge was being extensively quarried for building and road stone, and as Frank Knight concluded in *The Heart of Mendip* they "detracted in no inconsiderable degree from the charm and attraction of the place". In fact the public were so disturbed that sufficient money was collected to buy the quarries out, and transfer them to the sides of the road leading up to Shipham, where as we have seen they have sadly ruined two hills. If Frank Knight could have predicted that havoc, he would possibly not have been quite so sanguine about the scars that quarries leave behind them. "In time," he wrote, "no doubt, the scars that now disfigure the Gorge will come to wear a natural appearance, and will eventually appear to be merely a part of the cliffs themselves."

Fortunately Cheddar Gorge was virtually quarried by hand, and Knight's prophecy has come true. The threat to the Gorge went on, however, and it was only in 1928, when the Society of Somerset Folk (ancestors of the Somerset Trust for Nature Conservation and the Mendip Society) gave the cliffs to the National Trust, that it was finally averted.

In the east of the region, where the threat from the quarries is most acute today, people were complaining about them in the early nineteenth century. In 1823, Mrs Tuck, a Frome versifier, attacked the blasting in a quatrain whose feeling well makes up for any metrical oddities:

> Now all is still, save when the crash
> Of rifted crag with thundering dash
> From its huge bed of limestone flung
> Echoes tremendously and long.

It was after the war that the menace of the quarries accelerated. In the 1950s Herbert Balch, then in his eighties, led campaigns against the extensions of the quarries at Underwood and Dulcote, which had already made serious inroads into the hills around Wells. The scars left by those quarries; the gaping hole in the hillside above Cheddar, which almost dwarfs the famous Gorge; and the wholesale removal of hills in the east of the region would have horrified our ancestors, who believed that the quarrying of stone for essential building should always be done discreetly and with as little disturbance to the landscape as possible. Many farmers can show you the field out of which the stone for their farm buildings was taken, and often all that is visible is a slight dip in the field, or a shelter belt of trees, planted partly to hide the scar. In the eighteenth century the Court Leet of Mells spoke out against its "waywardens for digging up ye fore mentioned Quar on ye Green and not making provision to fill it in again". Both waywardens and private individuals were blamed for quarrying stone indiscriminately, yet that stone was at least being used for local roads, and not for those as far away as East Anglia, which is the case today. Nor did the local roads devour hills as fast as they do now. Crook Peak very nearly disappeared to make the M5, and was only saved when the people attending a public inquiry into the matter in November 1966 issued a stern rebuff to the proposal.

No such last-minute reprieve has come for the hills to the east of Wells. The ridge between Shepton Mallet and Frome is rapidly being eaten away, but from the main road it is the quarries between Merehead and Holwell that are the most obvious. A climb up to the hills from Doulting brings you to even worse disasters, with the whole village of Stoke St Michael practically obliterated. Further to the east, Whatley quarry has eaten right across the footpath that once ran from Railford Bridge to Mells. In common with many other deep quarries it has cut through several important springs and altered the water flow, in ways that are difficult to calculate or trace but whose effects are often inconvenient and damaging.

There is no such puzzle about dust. It is simply the most obvious, immediate and serious inconvenience that people living near the quarries have to face. It was dust that caused the great quarry rows of the 1960s, when the people in the villages to the east of Frome found that it was making their lives intolerable. In 1967, the Nunney cattle went sick as a result of it, and the stuff was penetrating the houses. Early morning traffic noise was added to the misery of the dust, for in 1968 a thousand quarry lorries were passing through Frome each day. The blasting was also becoming insufferable. People in Nunney had their windows shattered.

At this time, on the ridge to the south of Chantry, Redland Roadstone was trying to get permission to extend its quarry into the 240 acres of Bangle Farm, where a hard gritstone used for non-skid surfaces is found. The planning permission for the operation was finally rejected in November 1968. That welcome decision came as the result of a long and bitter struggle between the local residents and the developers; had the latter been successful another Mendip ridge would have totally disappeared.

Fortunately that battle was won, but the war goes on and the dust is still with us. And as well as polluting the air, quarrying can both pollute and disturb the water supply. In the days of the lead mining, armed men from Cheddar attacked the slaggers at the Charterhouse mineries, whom they accused of polluting the waters that came out of the hills above the town, so that they ran grey and the fish died in them. Those waters run clear now, but elsewhere the pollution goes on. St Dunstan's Well has been fouled with dust and slurry from the quarries of Stoke St Michael; Holwell rising has suffered from the dumping of whey in a nearby quarry; and Nunney Brook has been deoxygenated from the same cause.

In 1971 the Somerset County Council's quarry study predicted that by the year 2010, Mendip would be producing 60 million tons of limestone every year. That equals one sixth of one per cent of the limestone reserves of the hills. So twelve per cent would vanish in the average human lifespan. Already those figures are outdated. The quarrying goes on ever faster, and as the great crushers munch through the stone of Mendip the machines have become so internationally valued that the Shepton Mallet firm of Croft Impresa has managed to sell one to Peru. So when these hills have gone for ever, the Andes can be eaten away.

CHAPTER XII

Not Exactly: Mendip mysteries

"HE'S NOT ZACTLY" they say in north Somerset of anyone whose rational powers are a bit shaky. In that sense some of the stories about the places on Mendip are "not zactly", though they may contain the wisdom of the fool. The roots of the stories and of some of the customs with which they are associated lie in diverse soils from Victorian sentimentality to the rich stuff of prehistory and myth. They have flourished well here, for the hills were isolated for so long. Until the turn of the century wild miners, as well as the continual mists, kept the more orderly valley people, with their more clement weather, off the plateau.

It is to the nineteenth century that the tradition that Christ came to Mendip belongs. He is supposed to have been brought to Somerset by his uncle, Joseph of Arimathea, when the latter was on a trade visit to this country occasioned by the Cornish tin. As Mendip lead was also internationally acclaimed at that time, the proposition is not entirely impossible. However, the phrase "As sure as Our Lord walked on Priddy" is more quoted by the pious than believed by the inhabitants. Yet the attraction of the thought persists, and so a new legend is born and fostered by verses such as this which appeared in the Shipham parish magazine in 1982:

> The Son of Man on Mendip
> Gave the folk no sign
> But talked and walked with such as worked
> The lead and calamine.
> He knew the old nine barrows
> The swallets and the droves
> As well as on far southern slopes
> He knew the orange groves.

That hymn, if such it is, says in effect that all places are holy if they are properly attended to. The purpose of many annual customs is to enhance that attention, and to give the participants a feeling of belonging to a particular location and an identification with the people who live there. Such a spirit informs the Frome inter-denominational Sunday School processions, which started as an annual event in 1817, as well as more secular events like the New Year singing round the green which was once Banwell mill pond.

All seasonal festivals and ceremonies have their origins in the rhythms of agriculture; later more ephemeral customs grew out of such practical matters as the division of the land. The Dolemoors are a stretch of rough grazing on the northern levels near the village of Puxton. Before those moors were enclosed in 1811, the grazing was apportioned on the Saturday before midsummer day. The lots were drawn in the following manner. The land was divided into sections, and the turf of each marked with a different sign, similar patterns being cut into the skin of the same number of apples. Each tenant then plucked out an apple from a barrel and claimed the strip of ground that bore the corresponding mark.

That custom has died out, but the early-November carnivals of north Somerset, which touch Mendip at Wells and Shepton Mallet, grow in strength from year to year. The expensive, competing floats, which present the tableaux in lengthy carnival processions winding through the main streets of a different town each night for a week, follow a tradition started at the end of the last century. Most people have a feeling that it all has something to do with Guy Fawkes, and of course it has, but the junketings of November 5th are essentially linked to the fire rites with which the Celts celebrated their New Year, marked by the beginning of winter, and the slaughter of those cattle who could not be fed during the hungry months.

That necessary practice was remembered in the cruel sport of bull baiting. In Axbridge that barbaric custom went on as late as 1880. The bull victim was led out of the George Inn, goaded into racing up High Street and West Street to Outing Batch on Townsend Farm, where it was tied to the bull anchor and stoned to death. At least the meat was given to the poor.

Even more basic than the seasonal rites of agriculture is man's need for water. In a limestone area, where the rivers flow underground and the supply is unpredictable, it is no wonder that special attention should be paid to wells and springs. No one would describe the dowsers, or water-diviners, whose skills are still sometimes in demand, as being "not zactly". In fact, the folk belief is that to do his job effectively, a dowser must be in good health. A forked hazel or blackthorn branch is the traditional dowsing implement; but as the search depends on the small, involuntary muscles of the shoulders being activated by the presence of water, and so moving whatever is held loosely in the hands, almost any object will do to give the signal. A wire coat hanger can be used, and particularly sensitive people can even register the twitch above water without the need of any object to make a sign.

In contrast to Derbyshire, where wells are still regularly dressed and blessed, the Mendip risings are unhallowed. There are one or two possible exceptions, such as St Aldhelm's well at Doulting; but if a chapel had ever stood over the spring there, it had disappeared by the nineteenth century when John Farbrother was headmaster of Shepton Mallet school, but at least he had heard "of a late, learned divine, who was in the habit of walking thither from Shepton, regularly every morning, for the purpose of bathing his eyes, and whose sight was said to have been much benefited thereby". If that cure was true, then the Doulting well must have had much the same quality as Bully Well, Chew Magna, which was also acclaimed as being good for the eyes. At Pilton are two wells which were sanctified because pilgrims visited them on their way to Glastonbury. Their virtues appear to have been purely spiritual. However, in the village of Wellow, just outside Bath on the edge of Mendip, there is a lucky well. It is simply a spring of clear water in the hedgerow, and it was traditionally supposed to bring good fortune to anybody who drank its waters.

The caves from which the waters come have their own folklore. They say that the devil was responsible for the wretched dog who went into the cave at Goatchurch and came out at Burrington Coombe completely bald. Anyone familiar with the state of cavers' clothes could probably produce a less supernatural explanation for that, but the story of the disappearing fiddler is less easily argued away. This tale, which has parallels from all over Britain, concerns a fiddler from Priddy who vanished into a pit at Rookham. From that depth, he is supposed to reappear during severe thunderstorms, and lure people to their destruction with his sweet playing.

Herbert Balch thought it no wonder that Wookey Hole should be a ghost-haunted place to which parsons were once wont to condemn wandering spirits. He quoted Jenning's *Mysteries of Mendip* in evidence of that:

To lay the lorn spirit you o'er it must pray,
And command it at length to be gone far away,
And in Wookey's deep hole to be under control
For the space of seven years and a day.
If then it returns you must pray and command
At midnight, by moonlight, by Death's ebon wand,
That to Cheddar cliffs now it departeth in peace,
And another seven years its sore troubling will cease.

The most ghostly phenomena that Balch found in Wookey Hole were its noises. They were caused, he explained, by the air coming through the underground river in great bubbles. The sounds had an international fame as far back as the third century BC, when the Greek theologian, Clement of Alexandria, wrote of a certain cave in Britain, "at the side of a mountain, and at the entrance to a gap; where when the wind blows into the cave and is drawn on into the bosom of the interior, a sound is heard as of the clashing of numerous cymbals".

Balch was in no doubt that Clement's cave was Wookey Hole. He once heard even stranger sounds there. He was alone with his friend Captain Kentish, who was to be killed in the First World War and so unable to corroborate the account of their experience. As Balch told it, the two of them heard a chatter of voices, which they took to be another party of cavers on their way towards them. However, after a while the voices grew into a murmur and then into a roar, which expanded into an "overwhelming thunderous noise which enveloped us . . . then with painful suddenness it ceased". He could give no rational explanation for the experience.

Possibly what Balch heard was caused by a sudden change of water level somewhere in the depths of the hill. Above, as well as below ground, stories of strange noises abound; and that is not surprising when it is recorded that the sounds from the Cheddar factory that made the chip baskets for the strawberry harvest could be heard through a swallet in the fields where they were growing, a mile or more away up the hillside. In the early 1900s, one cottager in Cheddar's Lippiatt was certain that his house was haunted when the sound of horses' hooves echoed in his fireplace every afternoon between 4.30 and 5 p.m. It turned out to be the clatter of the coal carts coming back along the top of the hill from Midsomer Norton, and the sound was transmitted through underground rifts in the limestone.

Ghostly or not, the caves have always attracted strange tales and speculations. One tells of a hound who went into Cooper's Hill (by the car park in Cheddar Gorge) and came out at Wookey Hole. Even more fascinating is the story of the vast underground Cheddar lake with man-made steps leading down to it, which Gough's son heard of from an old man who had lived in the Gorge for many years. Its entrance is supposed to be behind Long hole Cave, a place long silted up with debris from the lead mines.

As Jenning's lines tell us, Cheddar cliffs were likely to be as ghost-ridden as its caves, with real creatures also acting as agents of doom. When bird-nesting was an acceptable pastime, no one hesitated to collect hawks' eggs from the cliffs, while those of the raven were left strictly alone. An old villager told Frank Knight that when a local ornithologist shot two of those powerful birds, he was only able to find one. Moreover, it was not long before he took ill and died. The evil propensity of ravens is accentuated in the following sinister lullaby, in which the black birds of doom are contrasted with the more homely sparrows and magpies:

> Hush a bye babby, th' baggers shan't ha' thee
> No more shall th' maggotty pie.
> But th' rooks and th' ravens shall car thee to hebben
> Singing "Lullabye, Lullabye-bye".

Churches, which are supposed to keep people safe from such portents, collect their own folklore. Uphill church stands where it does, on the crest of a hill, a steep climb from the village, because St Nicholas, to whom the church is dedicated, was determined that it should not be built by the houses on the levels. Every night he dismantled the builders' work and took the building materials up to the site he had chosen. Perhaps he did so because as patron saint of sailors he felt it would be more useful if his church tower could be used as a landmark.

However, if those sailors perished as they struggled through the treacherous currents of the Bristol Channel, as did those from the boat that was swept up channel from Lundy in the early 1900s, and whose hull still rests on Burnham sands, they would not necessarily be given a churchyard burial. Until 1870, it was on the tide line that sailors were buried, not in the churchyards of St Nicholas at Uphill or St Bridget at Brean. Even when they were allowed on consecrated ground, their bodies were kept in a separate sailors' graveyard in case the sea should reclaim them, and some token was buried at the water's edge to stop their spirits walking. A Brean song, collected by Ruth Tongue in 1900, reflects that custom:

The waters they washed 'en ashore, ashore,
And they never will sail the seas no more.
We laid 'en along by the churchyard wall
And all in a row we buried them all.
But their boots we buried below the tide
On Severn Side.

Unlike in the Quantocks, where dragons abound, I have only found one good and ancient Mendip worm. It is a rather friendly-looking creature for all it has a head at each end. It was found in three pieces in the chancel wall of Dinder's medieval church when it was being restored in 1872. The creature, which dates from a very much earlier chapel, which stood on the site long before Dinder became a parish, now rests above the rector's stall.

Quite properly it is the cathedral at Wells that has collected the greatest store of Mendip miracles. People suffering from toothache were often relieved by prayers at the tomb of Bishop William Bitten, who died in 1267. The cynical may say that those cures depended as much on the pun as on divine intervention; but no such explanation can hold for the healing powers of William de Marchia, who died in 1293 and who is buried between the door of the cloisters and the altar of St Martin.

The most miraculous event to take place in Wells was related to Isaac Casaubon by no less reliable a source than the great Elizabethan prelate, Lancelot Andrews, Bishop of Ely, who had the story from Bishop Still of Bath and Wells. One summer day in 1596, two claps of thunder so astounded the people at divine service in the cathedral, that they all fell on their knees. Lightning was seen, and although nobody was hurt, everyone present was marked with the imprint of the cross.

Special providence, rather than a miracle, was responsible for the preservation of the life of the holy Bishop, Thomas Ken, on the very night that his successor at Wells, Bishop Kidder, was killed with his wife when the ceiling of the palace collapsed on them during the great storm of November 26th 1703 at the time of the Wells Cloth Fair. Ken was staying in Salisbury at that time, and very nearly died in a similar fashion. He described his escape to William Lloyd, Bishop of

Norwich, telling him that when workmen came to assess the damage after the storm, they found "that the beam which supported the roof over my head was shaken out to that degree, that it had but half an inch to hold together, for which signal and particular preservation God's holy name be ever praised".

Good men like Ken and Kidder have not returned to confuse the living, but Mendip has had its share of ghostly happenings. Old Beecham of Sidcot school had a reputation for being a bit of a wizard and a conjuror. His magic staff, red cap and volumes of books were signs of his calling; and he was consulted on all sorts of ills for he even had a reputation as a cow doctor. When he came to die, he expressed a wish to be buried in his own garden. It was not granted, and being discontented with his churchyard grave he returned to earth in the form of a poltergeist on the first anniversary of his death, which fell on July 22nd 1789. All his widow's possessions were thrown about the cottage, and when the elders from the Quaker meeting were called in to the scene of the confusion, they were greeted by a heavy armchair which came to meet them of its own accord. Even Hannah More and the rector of Shipham, who visited the place soon afterwards, were baffled by the phenomenon.

Some similar story might account for the strange behaviour of one of the leaded windows at Lower Farm, Charterhouse, where Walter Raymond is supposed to have written his best-loved novel, *Two Men o' Mendip*. Tradition has it that in the Middle Ages, nine lay brothers from Witham Friary, which had grazing rights on the hills, made their home here. A farmhouse for centuries, the building has now been lovingly restored by a Bristol architect and his wife, yet one window overlooking Longwood remains obdurate. No matter how often they are replaced there are always two cracked panes in that casement.

Mendip heights in autumn mists are eerie, and it is not surprising that the lane which runs by Priddy Nine Barrows on North Hill and the one going past Lamb Leer cavern to East Harptree are both ghost-ridden. People try to avoid walking, or even driving along them, and I've heard it said that "it's almost as though people do be peeking over the hedge at you".

Other hauntings are more personal. The lady who died in mysterious circumstances at Winterhead Manor House is said to return to her old home; and so does a young First World War widow, who lived briefly with her husband at the top of St Thomas's Street in

Wells. Her story is made all the more poignant by the fact that the marriage was strongly disapproved of by the young man's wealthy parents.

Mendip's most saintly ghost is that of the British monk, Gildas, who retreated to Steep Holm in the sixth century to write his complaint about the downfall of Britain. Rodney Legg of the Kenneth Allsop Trust, which administers the island, says that the story that the monk's footsteps can still be heard there is nothing but a Victorian invention. Kenneth Cass, the Trust's engineer, believes otherwise. He has not personally heard Gildas walking, but he has seen apparitions by the site of the old priory. The first time that he was aware of the spirits was early one summer afternoon in 1980, when he saw four monk-like figures watching the archaeologists at work. The following summer he saw the shadowy figures again, and could not resist telling the people on the dig that they were being watched. One replied, "Yes, I know they're there, but I can't see them."

Suicides are said to return to the crossroads where they lie buried as frequently on Mendip as elsewhere. The word "Grave" in a place name can well be a corruption of "Grove", yet many stories have grown up about the Cannard, who is supposed to lie beneath Cannard's Grave outside Shepton Mallet, at a crossroads, first recorded by that name in the parish bounds of 1692. Apparently at this rather shabby road junction there was once a great coaching inn, successfully managed by one Giles Cannard, whose greed led him into many questionable transactions. When these were discovered his fear of ruin drove him to suicide, according to one story, and to his hanging, according to another.

At Woodspring to the north of Weston-super-Mare there is another crossroads associated with both a suicide and illegal trading. They say that four ghostly men came to that spot to attempt to give the suicide beneath it a proper burial, and that it is certain death for any living soul to try and watch them at their work. That was a crafty threat, for the brandy smuggled in from Kewstoke was often carried inland in coffins.

No such easy and rational explanations offer themselves for the tales that have collected round the ordinary little town of Shepton Mallet. Joseph Glanvil of nearby Frome, who was writing between 1661 and 1680, complained that it was a place where witches and wizards were thick on the ground. But it was their master, the devil, who has been held responsible for the later mysterious disappearance of the ancient and crippled Owen Parfitte, who vanished from his chair outside his sister's house between six and seven one June evening in 1763.

Another person to go missing from Shepton Mallet in the eighteenth century was Nancy Camel. That old lady lived alone and earned her bread by knitting stockings and selling woad and teazles to the weavers. Like many another such solitary creature she acquired a reputation as a witch. That was enhanced when, after a fearful storm in the 1870s, no trace of her could be found in the cave in the rock face (just above the site of the present sewage works) where she had made her home. The wheel and hoof marks on the threshold of her wretched shelter were proof enough that the devil had come for his own. The story was not weakened when, in 1888, a Dr Allen excavated the place and found traces of the old woman's habitation; although a few years before that the old man who told the tale of Nancy to John Farbrother added the rider that "Shepton people be so wicked, there be no knowing how true it be".

Before poor Nancy's time, witch-hunting was as rife at Shepton as anywhere else in England. Joseph Glanvil chronicled many of the cases and took part in the witch-hunts, in pursuit of his own philosophical speculations on the supernatural, and in defence of his creed that belief in God was inconsistent with a disbelief in embodied evil. Chronicling the supernatural powers of Jane Brooks, he related how that old woman induced fits in twelve-year-old Richard Jones in the winter of 1657. On February 25th the next year, according to Glanvil's account, she caused the lad to levitate in the garden of Richard Isles' house in Shepton Mallet, and had him mount so high that he rose above the garden wall to fall, as though dead, more than 30 yards the other side of it. Jane was executed at Chard on March 26th.

Can one associate a saint and a witch in one story? If so, one of the earliest traditions of Mendip witchcraft centres on the person of St Wigefort, to whom St Andrew's church at Chew Stoke was once dedicated. She was commonly known as Maid Uncumber, for the story goes that as the Christian daughter of the heathen king of Portugal she fought her parents' demand that she marry a heathen prince. In order to be saved from such a fate, she prayed that her body might be made repellent. Promptly she grew a beard, and that so angered her father that he at once ordered her to be crucified. As a martyr she takes care of those virgins who suffer for refusing a man for any legitimate reason; and she earned her name of "uncumber" by her willingness, in urgent cases, to rid wives of unwanted husbands. To obtain that favour, women had to make her an offering of wild oats.

Such procedures may seem dubious, but at least one Mendip white witch was a real saint. In 1555 Elizabeth Page of Blagdon was asked to cure a little girl who was desperately ill. She simply looked at the child and made no comment. Later she explained that in order to effect a cure, she had to cause herself to be as ill as the sick person. In the same year the Wells Diocesan Records relate that John Tucie of Banwell was accused of sorcery on May 16th, and that one Joan Tyrry was claiming that she got secret knowledge from the fairies. Meanwhile a wizard of Wells was claiming to have cured over a hundred people of the ague by giving them an abracadabra acrostic to wear.

The last recorded fatal ducking of an old lady accused of being a witch took place in the notorious Woodland district of Frome in 1731, but a belief in witchcraft persisted for well over a century after that. In 1867, the Reverend Charles Foster of Chewton Mendip complained to the Parliamentary Commission on the employment of children in agriculture that in his parish "if anyone has a fit or the cow gives no milk, they consider they have been overlooked and send to the wise woman in Bristol". And at the beginning of this century Frank Knight related the tale of a Mendip man who shot at a white rabbit, but never managed to retrieve it. When he got home, an old woman who was suspected of being a black witch was found with her arm in a sling.

In contrast to the complexities of the witches' activities, much of the devil's work on Mendip seems to have been the simple matter of hurling stones about, and not very successfully at that. The two stones which he aimed at East Harptree church landed up in a field near Showle Farm; and he lost his most famous throwing match. That took place on Shute Shelve against Mendip's giant, Sir John Hautville, who lived in the thirteenth century and who is thought to have been buried in the vanished church of Norton Hawkfield, although there is a fifteenth-century effigy of him at Chew Magna. Hautville won his contest with the devil by two furlongs, but the devil's stone was four times larger and can still be seen in the fields at Cross opposite Burton Lane. That probably pleases the devil well enough. He also had a bit of good fortune at Banwell, when he frustrated the attempt to put up a stone cross in the village by constantly blowing it over. So the villagers had to resort to digging a cruciform earthwork on the top of Banwell hill, and certainly there seems to be no other explanation for that odd formation.

Yet it could be that the Banwell cross, like Gorsey Bigbury, the many barrows and the few standing stones of Mendip, has a very ancient pagan origin. When men first settled on these hills, sheltering in the limestone caves and making clearings in the woods, they must have turned, as men have always done since that time, to some superhuman agency to defend them against the threats of warring tribes, wild beasts, harsh weather, famine and disease. Many unexplained monuments relate to that need.

The feeling for the supernatural has always been at war with ordinary human greed. Legends of buried treasure became attached to the hilltop barrows where the chieftains of Bronze Age tribes were buried, and persisted for centuries. A golden coffin is supposed to lie under the earth in the neighbourhood of the round barrows on Beacon Hill; another in the Murty Hill long barrow at Buckland Dinham, which is said to be haunted by a lady in white; and a third in one of the barrows near Smalldown Camp by Evercreech. Their existence has never been proved for tomb robbery is traditionally cursed. That belief is borne out by the stone near a tumulus at Binegar which brings bad luck to anyone who tries to move it. The last attempt was made by a tenant farmer in 1905. He took four horses to the task, but they could not shift the stone, and his unsuccessful attempt was followed by a string of personal disasters.

It is as true on Mendip as elsewhere, that as tumuli are traditionally regarded as ill-fated places of buried treasure, so stone circles are petrified Sabbath breakers, a legend which could have arisen from their use for the Sabbats of covens of witches. However that may be, on the 1736 map of Somerset, the red stones of Stanton Drew are marked as The Weddings, and the story goes that a Saturday wedding party once danced in those fields by the River Chew. At midnight, at the approach of the holy time, the fiddler grew apprehensive, but the groom, at the bride's insistence, said that he intended to go on dancing, if the devil himself had to play. Immediately a new, unknown piper appeared.

The story is as improbable as the one that Stanton Drew's outrider, a single recumbent stone on the other side of the river, by the main road to Bristol, was thrown there from Maes Knoll by the redoubtable Hautville. Yet there is no way of knowing what really went on in that complex of stones which form the second largest ritual site in Britain after Avebury. The seemingly haphazard arrangement of the stones has given rise to the belief that, like those that make up the Rollright circle in Oxfordshire, they are uncountable; and that anyone who so much as attempts to do so is likely to be struck dead.

That belief could be a warning that the mysterious origins of this place are best left unprobed by anyone who would experience the gentle peace of the place over which the stones preside. They are on private land and have now to be approached through a working farmyard, and ironically cannot be reached at all on the Sabbath. That slight inconvenience links this ancient monument to the present necessities of an area of which they were once the spiritual centre.

EPILOGUE

Preserving the Hills

MY EXPLORATION OF Mendip started on a March day on the rocky, limestone humps of Brean Down. Now it is dank January, nearly two years later, and I walk far inland among the 400-year-old remains of open-cast coal mining. A scrubby wood has grown up in the disturbed ground, an outlying hazel houses a colony of long-tailed tits, and in the midst of the trees I am delighted and surprised by a kingfisher darting up from a black, stagnant pool into which some of the water from Mells stream was drained during the mining operations.

Edford Wood is a swampy place, clearly of no use to its owner but full of delight for the naturalist, despite the death of much of the water. It is a place of man-made islands linked by new plank bridges and ancient drainage systems beside the clear and fast-flowing river. Yew, box and the encroaching rhododendron grow among the ash and oak, and in spring the undergrowth is filled with wild daffodils.

In the valley to the south of the wood are the ruined fragments of the settlement at Stoke Bottom; the fields to the north carry traces of the failed Somerset Coal Canal; and beyond that, over the hill and through the modern village, is the isolated church that once served the lost cottages of Holcombe. A quarry flanks the eastern edge of the wood, and the noise of its operation breaks the still silence of winter.

This little area is a microcosm of Mendip now, a palimpsest of the active past of an area from the Middle Ages to the nineteenth century, richly serving the interests of both historian and naturalist. A museum piece, the cruel might say, as they wait for the neighbouring quarry to eat through the hills and coombs. That is a harsh judgement, but one which anyone who is serious about conservation has to consider. How is it possible to achieve a balance between the demands of modern technology and the established character and natural ecology of the hills? In east Mendip the question is particularly stark.

Obviously the only answer can come from wise administration. Both Brean Down and Edford Wood lie in Somerset, although as the county boundary follows the course of the River Axe, Brean only just comes under that authority. To the north the hills belong to Avon. As far as Mendip is concerned the interests of these two county councils often conflict. To Somerset the hills mean farms and quarries; for the over-populated conurbations of Bristol and Bath they are a leisure resource, to which, in the words of Tom Elkin, the newly appointed warden of the Mendip Hills, "they feel they have some God-given right".

Somehow these main uses of the land have to be brought into harmony in ways that will preserve, or at least not too rapidly destroy, the essential character of the hills.

The matter is complicated by a second division, partly geological, which differentiates between western Mendip, designated an Area of Outstanding Natural Beauty, and the sacrificed eastern hills. As long as that situation exists most of the active work concerned with the practical conservation of the hills takes place in the west. The best one can hope for is that the work that is now being done there will serve as a good model should the A.O.N.B. ever be extended to Vallis Vale near Frome, as it ought to be.

Mr Elkin, a former teacher and warden of Somerset Education Committee's field centre at Charterhouse for sixteen years, took up his new post in September 1983. His responsibilities cover an area of 64 square miles, from Hutton in the west to West Horrington in the east, and from Cheddar in the south to Bishop Sutton on the edge of Chew Valley Lake in the north. One of his many functions is to ensure that ten miles of green lanes and nearly a thousand miles of bridleways and footpaths in that region are properly maintained and way-marked.

The territory also includes several large quarries whose existence pre-dates the area's special designation, but which no authority can afford to buy off. At least the Somerset County Council has ceased work at its own Underwood quarry above Wells, but as I write there is a scheme for its crushing equipment to be used for rendering slag from South Wales into tarmac. The projected increase in heavy traffic that would bring about, and the subsequent over-burdening of roads already strained to their limits, is horrific enough to galvanize a fairly acquiescent population into demands for a public inquiry.

The politics raised by the quarries are outside Tom Elkin's brief. His hands are full enough with the task of trying to balance the needs of land owners and visitors. In order to do so, he is trying to provide both the safeguards and amenities that are procured in other areas by the provision of a National Park. For although Mendip does not have that status, he is setting out to provide the sort of information and services that visitors to Exmoor and Dartmoor have come to expect.

For this purpose he has a team of volunteer wardens whose main task is to help people to make the best of their excursions to the hills and to understand enough about the nature of the land and its use to treat it with respect. Each warden has a special district to patrol, but although the popular image is of some pseudo-policeman ordering motorcyclists off footpaths, that is far from being their main function.

Indeed, Tom Elkin considers that the bugbear of the motorcyclists, whom he finds in the main to be perfectly reasonable youngsters, can be an exaggerated threat to the hills. He is far more worried about the way that the horses from the numerous riding schools churn up the bridleways beyond redemption. The combination of Mendip rain and strings of eight horses or more, going out regularly throughout the day for the customary hour's ride from the seven riding schools in Shipham alone, has turned many a Rowberrow track into a swamp.

In the main the riding schools cater for the visitors from the towns, but horses can be equally destructive in the hands of people who live on the hill. Lady Sarah Wright, daughter of Lord Waldegrave and thus a member of one of the oldest of the great land-owning families on Mendip, claims that "a newly planted wood can look like Passchendæle after the hunt has been through it".

To the casual observer the most unsightly things on any stretch of open country are the cars with which the visitors wreck the views that they have come out to see. Tom Elkin, who has counted as many as 186 cars by Priddy Pools alone, would like to solve the problem by setting up "honey pot" car parking areas as many of the National Parks have done; choosing the most popular and accessible beauty spots and encouraging people to use them to the exclusion of other parts of the hills by setting up refreshment and toilet facilities nearby.

Although he is aware that few visitors to the country feel secure enough to stray far from their cars, he hopes to encourage even "honey pot" motorists to take an intelligent interest in the places they have chosen to visit. So as well as planning a full-scale information centre at Charterhouse, he hopes to set up interpretative points manned by voluntary wardens at the car parks; and even to arrange for guided walks to start from such places. Ideally he would like to run a mini-bus service, like the one that operates in some parts of the Lake District.

This would mean that some areas of the hills could be cut off to visitors' cars completely, leaving them open to walkers and to those people who made use of the bus service from the car parks.

Such an arrangement would both preserve the hills and increase the discerning visitor's enjoyment. Over and over again, Tom Elkin stresses the pleasure that comes from understanding what you see. He is still primarily interested in education in its widest sense, and much of his work consists in liaising with parish councils, the various conservation bodies and the local schools in an endeavour to help the thousands of people who come to Mendip to understand the life of the hills. This practical "education" must take the form of field trips and guided walks, which pose their own administrative problems. When one was recently advertised by Radio Bristol, 170 people turned out for it. To avoid that sort of embarrassment in future some sort of booking system will probably have to be arranged.

Walkers apart, the sheer numbers of visitors to the Mendip region each year is staggering. Even cavers have been known to queue up to get underground, while hundreds of thousands of coaches bring the tourists to the show caves. Even the more genteel pleasure of a stroll round the gardens of the Bishop's Palace in Wells attracts around 33,000 people each year. At least the eastern end of the hills is saved from that sort of onslaught.

Tourism is Somerset's second industry, agriculture its main one. The conservationists are all well aware that whatever provisions they make are dependent on the co-operation of farmers and land owners. Lady Sarah, an enthusiastic and knowledgeable botanist, is worried at the way that new methods of intensive arable farming can damage the very frail Mendip topsoil; and she is concerned about the effects of the massive accumulation of untreated slurry as the size of the herds of cattle continues to increase.

Farming practices can change a landscape almost as completely, if not as permanently, as quarrying. Now that fewer sheep graze the uplands the hills are rapidly reverting to scrub in many places, so that the ridge of Blackdown which was once green pasture is now brown with bracken and gorse and gives the impression of wild moorland. Yet that appearance is illusory. There is no truly wild land on Mendip, nor any public land if it comes to that. There is an owner for every half-acre of the hills, and the only people who have any rights to the common lands are those who live around them. Fortunately in many instances the naturalist trusts and conservation bodies are able to work with the land owners to ensure that the natural ecology and character of the hills are preserved. A particulatly happy example of that is the edge of the hill above Rowberrow which includes Dolebury hill fort. This is owned by the National Trust, managed by the Avon Wildlife Trust and sub-let to farmers for grazing sheep and cattle.

Below the hill fort are the conifers of Rowberrow Forest. On Mendip, as elsewhere, these commercial woodlands, whether in the accountable hands of the Forestry Commission or more frighteningly in the grasp of the owners of "dedicated" woodlands, where the land is exempt from any kind of planning control, have completely changed the landscape within a generation. The change is accentuated where the elms have disappeared and many old windbreaks which were landmarks for decades have gone. It will take years for the broad-leaf tree-planting operations that are going on now to make good that loss; but several projects are going ahead on Mendip and Somerset County Council considers them important enough to make a 50 per cent grant to land owners towards the cost of settling new trees.

Despite such generosity we do not tend to love our administrators and planners, knocking them as much for what they omit to restrain as for the restrictions which we feel they impose on individual freedom. On Mendip poor or non-existent planning has led to the destruction of many a skyline, with rows of mediocre buildings lined up along the ridge of a hill in order to provide the occupants with a good view no matter what anyone else has to put up with. In general there is often more encouragement to develop land for new buildings than to restore those that are already there, and in many places this has led to rashes of ugly and inappropriate suburban bungalows.

In farm buildings, too, the lack of planning and control often leads to the destruction of a landscape. In a dairy, stock-rearing area there must be silos for winter feeds, and no one minds that insignia of a working farm. The misfortune is in the creation of unsightly corrugated iron buildings, put up at the rate of 5,000 square feet every two years, with no planning permission at all required; while ancient stone barns that could be completely workable are deliberately allowed to fall into ruin, in many cases having their roofs removed to hasten the process.

There have to be changes, and for most people and in many ways the changes on the hills since the war have been for the better. No one would want to go back to the 1930s, when farm labourers' wages were 30s a week, and Lord Waldegrave kept a rabbit warren at Priddy to supplement his workers' larders; or even to the 1940s and '50s when many homes still lacked piped water. It is easy to be romantic about the "countryside", a word that Lady Sarah hates, for she claims that it has about as much to do with the real country as the word "seaside" has to do with the sea.

Like the sea, the country is not always comfortable. For years the harsh weather of Mendip made this largest island to rise out of the Somerset levels a wild, isolated place that most people tried to avoid. Now all that has changed, the two hilltop settlements of Priddy and Hinton Blewitt are spreading, and houses are constantly being built on the lower slopes.

Mendip is country still. It is an area of enormous variety whose essential character is embodied in the very rocks of its structure, as the artist Peter Coates discovered twenty years ago when he turned from abstract to landscape painting through a fascination with the shapes of the stones from Mendip's screes and walls. As Mendip gave him his vocation it is mostly these hills that he paints, being most stimulated by them as a "winter landscape". He is right. Beautiful in all seasons, Mendip is most itself on a bright, still winter's day, sharp enough to deter the hordes of casual visitors. Indeed Mendip weather is in some ways an ally to the conservationists; but despite the late springs and frequent mists, it will take enormous funds of goodwill and intelligence to prevent these country hills becoming swamped by suburban countryside.

BIBLIOGRAPHY

Atthill, Robin (ed.): *Mendip: A new study*, David and Charles, 1976
    : *Old Mendip*, David and Charles, 1964
    : *The Curious Past*, West Country Studies, 1955
Balch, H. E.: *Mendip — The Great Cave of Wookey Hole*, Cathedral Press, 1929
Barrington, Nicholas and Stanton, William: *Mendip: The Complete Caves and a View of the Hills*, Cheddar Valley Press, 1976
Bedford, Bruce: *Challenge Underground*, Allen & Unwin, 1975
Belham, Peter: *The Making of Frome*, 1973
Bettey, J. H. (ed.): *Chew Magna and District in 1851*, Bristol University, 1973
Billingsley, John: *General View of Agriculture in the County of Somerset*, 1795
Birmingham, George: *Pleasant Places* (Mells), 1934
Cassan, Stephen Hyde: *Bishops of Bath and Wells*, C & J Rivington, 1829
Cleverden, Rev. F. W.: *A History of Mells* ed. Michael McGarvie, 1974
Clew, Kenneth R.: *The Dorset and Somerset Canal*, David & Charles, 1971
    : *The Somersetshire Coal Canal and Railways*, David & Charles, 1970
Collinson, Rev. John: *History and Antiquities of Somerset*, 1791
Compton, Theodore: *A Mendip Valley*, Edward Stanford (London) 1892
Dobson, D. P.: *Archaeology of Somerset*, 1931
Down, C. G. and Warrington, A. J.: *History of the Somerset Coalfields*, David & Charles, 1971
Dunning Robert W.: *A History of Somerset*, Somerset County Library, 1978
Easton Ladies Guild: *Yesterday in Easton*, 1980
Farbrother, John E.: *Shepton Mallet*, C. A. Bartlett, 1872
Findlay, D. C.: *The Soils of the Mendip District of Somerset*, Harpenden, 1965

Fowles, John (Intro): *Steep Holm*, Kenneth Allsop Memorial Trust. Distributed: Dorset Publishing Company, 1978

Gough, J. W.: *The Mines of Mendip*, David & Charles, 1967

Greswell, William H. P.: *Forests and Deer Parks of Somerset*, Barnicott and Pearce (Taunton), 1905

Hadfield, C.: *The Canals of South-West England*, David and Charles, 1967

Hall, W. G. (ed.): *Man and the Mendips*, Mendip Society, 1971

Hallam, Olive: *The NFU in Somerset*, Somerset County Branch of the NFU, 1971

Hembry, Phyliss: *The Bishops of Bath and Wells. 1540–1640*, 1967

Hendy, E. W.: *Somerset Birds and Some other Folk*, Eyre & Spottiswoode, 1943

Hobhouse, Edmund (ed.): *Claver Morris: Diary of a West Country Physician 1684–1726*, Simpkin Marshall, 1934

Horne, Dom Ethelbert: *Idylls of Mendip*, Somerset Folk Press, 1922

Hudson, Kenneth: *The Bath and West*, Moonraker Press, 1976

Hylton, H. G. H., 3rd Baron: *Notes on the History of the Parish of Kilmersdon*, 1910

Knight, Frank: *History of Sidcot School. 1808–1908*
    : *The Heart of Mendip*, 1915 (Republished, Chatford House Press, Bristol, 1971)
    : *The Seaboard of Mendip*, J. M. Dent & Co, 1902

McGarvie, Michael: *Nunney and Trudoxhill*, 1977
    : *The Book of Frome*, Barracuda Books, 1980

Palmer, Kingsley: *The Folklore of Somerset*, Batsford, 1976

Parfitt, A. J.: *My Life as a Somerset Miner*, Miners' Office Radstock, 1930

Pearce, Susan M.: *The Kingdom of Domnonia*, Lodenek Press/Padstow, 1978

Phelp, William: *History and Antiquities of Somersetshire*, 1836

Poole, C. H.: *Customs, Superstitions and Legends of Somerset*, Sampson Low, 1877 (Republished, Toucan Press, Guernsey, 1970)

Porter, H. M.: *The Celtic Church in Somerset*, Morgan Books, 1971

Reid, R. D.: *Some Buildings of Mendip*, The Mendip Society, 1979

Rice, Hugh A. L.: *Thomas Ken: Bishop and non-juror*, SPCK, 1958

Richardson, L.: *Wells and Springs of Somerset*, HMSO, 1928

Roberts, Evelyn: *A Sidcot Pageant*, J. M. Dent, 1935

Rogers, Kenneth: *Wiltshire and Somerset woollen mills*, Pasold Research Fund Ltd, 1976

Rutter, John: *Delineation of the North West Division of Somerset*, 1829

Skinner, John: *Journal of a Somerset Rector, 1803–1834* (ed. Peter and Howard Coombs), Kingsmead, Bath, 1930 (revised 1971)

Somerset County Council: *Quarrying in Somerset*, County Planning Dept., Taunton, 1971

Stanton, W. I.: *Pioneer Under the Mendips: Biography of H. E. Balch*, Wessex Cave Club, 1969

Tate, William J.: *Somerset in Bygone Days*, Simpkin Marshall, 1912

Tongue, Ruth L.: *The Chime Child or Somerset Singers*, Routledge, 1967

Vowles, W.: *Hannah More and her friends, 1745–1833*, Downside Review, Vols LXX & LXI, 1942/43

Woodward, Geoffrey H.: *The Dissolution of the Chantries in the county of Somerset*, University of Bristol (Master's Degree), 1980

Fiction

Brock, Lynn: *The Mendip Mystery*, 1929

Goudge, Elizabeth: *City of Bells*, 1936

Hardy, Thomas: *Our Exploits at West Poley*, 1883

Hollis, Gertrude: *A Tale of Wells in the Days of Bishop Ken*, Clare Son & Co. Ltd., Wells, (Undated)

Mansfield, Estrith: *Gallows Close* (Monmouth novel), Stockwell (Ilfracombe), 1952

Marshall, Emma: *Under the Mendips*, Seeley & Co (London), 1891

Mathers, Helen: *Comin' Thro' the Rye*, (Chantry School), Collins, 1857

Raymond, Walter: *Two Men o' Mendip*, Somerset Folk Press, London, 1923

Tanner, Janet: *The Black Mountains*, Macdonald, 1981, Futura, 1983

INDEX

Bridgwater, 40, 61
Bristol, xviii, 17, 34, 36, 40, 45,
 54
Bristol Billy, 86
Bristol Channel, 3
Bristol Turnpike Trust, 57
Bristol Waterworks, 42, 47, 87,
 133
British Printing Corporation, 106
Bromwich, David, 61
Bronze Age, xvii, xviii, 4, 9, 55, 64,
 80, 118, 151
Brooks, Jane, 149
Brunel, Isambard Kingdom, 61
Bruton, 54
Bubwith, Nicholas, Bishop, 67
Buckland Dinham, 33, 60, 61, 112
Burnham-on-Sea, 124, 134, 144
Burrington Combe, xvi, 64, 86, 114,
 117, 120, 143
Burrows, E. B., 121
Butcher, Bill, 129, 130
Butler and Tanner, 106
Butt, John, 13

Cadmium, 83, 84
Callow Hill, 38, 52, 55, 58, 74, 80, 84,
 94, 132
Calomine, 31
Camel, Nancy, 149
Camerton, 33, 49, 60, 124
Camerton and Limpley Stoke Rail-
 way, 62
Canals, 59ff
Cannards Grave, 148
Carthusians, 31
Cass, Kenneth, 148
Castle Cary, 16
Castle of Comfort, 55, 64, 86
Catholics, 72
Cattle, cattlemen, xvii, 4, 5, 8, 9, 13,
 14, 17, 31, 139
Caves, caving, xvi, xix, 115ff, 121ff,
 156
Celts, Celtic, xiii, xvii, 52, 64, 81,
 111, 112, 118, 142
Chantry, 48, 107, 110, 139
Charles II, 34

Charterhouse, xviii, 4, 22, 23, 26, 27,
 28, 29, 31, 32, 48, 52, 53, 56, 68,
 75, 81, 82, 83, 87, 119, 129, 130,
 131, 139, 154, 155
Charterhouse Field Centre, 28, 154
Cheddar, xviii, 13, 16, 47, 53, 54, 56,
 57, 59, 62, 72, 79, 84, 89, 90, 91,
 95ff, 102, 112, 120, 121, 122, 132,
 138, 139, 144, 154
Cheddar Gorge, xvi, 32, 52, 90, 96ff,
 129, 131, 137, 138, 144
Cheddar Valley, 37, 41, 61, 62, 63, 98,
 99, 116, 120, 121
Cheese, 18, 19ff, 36, 97ff
Chew Magna, 20, 37, 54, 68, 87, 143,
 150
Chew, River, 3, 4, 45, 47, 64, 151
Chew Stoke, 16, 64, 68, 70, 106,
 149
Chew Valley/Chew Valley Lake, xix,
 7, 10, 44, 57, 87, 120, 132, 133,
 135, 154
Chewton, 19, 26
Chewton Mendip, 3, 4, 5, 8, 31, 49,
 97, 119, 150
Chilcompton, 113
Churchill, 54
Cider, 7, 105
Cloford, 11, 53, 136
Cloth, clothiers, 45ff, 110, 112
Coal, coal mining, xvii, 32ff, 59, 60,
 81, 86, 105, 106, 153
Coates, Peter, 158
Cobbett, William, 103, 110
Coleford, 36, 54, 58
Coleridge, S. T., 113
Collinson, John, 33, 44, 54, 83, 85,
 113
Compton Bishop, 56, 68, 91, 94
Compton Martin, xiii, 27, 30, 56, 66,
 68, 75, 119
Compton Theodore, 44, 62, 73
Congresbury, 4, 51, 65, 66, 68
Cornwell, John, 47
Cottle's Ash/Oak, 112
Cowslip Green, 79, 80
Cox, Richard, 116, 121
Crafts, 19